Just

What

the

Ph.D.

Ordered

FreeWillPublishers
Trussville, AL

Published by Freewill Publishers, Trussville, AL
Freewill Publishers also publishes its books in a variety of electronic formats.
For general information on other products and services, please e-mail
info@freewillpublishers.com or go to www.freewillpublishers.com

Originally published by Sparenot Publishers in 2006

Printed in the United States of America

Cover concept and design: Guru Graphics, Inc.

ISBN 978-0-9848667-3-1

ISBN (eBook) 978-0-9848667-6-2

Editor: Christie Woods

Library of Congress Control Number: 2013954862

Contents

ACKNOWLEDGEMENTS

There have been important people in my life, but none more important than my wife Angel Jones. As I complete the second edition of this book, she continues to be by my side in my work, my travels, and as my mate. I could not have experience success in graduate school without her. My wife has been there to keep me encouraged and grounded, so for that, she deserves much praise in helping me to complete this second edition of this book. We succeeded at this project together.

Also, I want to acknowledge our four beautiful children, Samiyah, Samuel II, Seth, and Saxton. At the time of the first print of this book, we had only two children (Samiyah and Samuel), but now we have added to our family with two more boys. My kids in their own little ways inspire and motivate me to keep striving.

Preface

I am more than excited about the second edition of my book. My ultimate goal for writing this second edition is to continue to have an impact on the reader's success in graduate school and in your personal life. You see, all of us have challenges. We don't have to relive events that many have already learned from. We can succeed by learning from others. That's the goal of the book.

An effective way to gain insight into a book is to gain insight into the author's experience, life, and way of thinking. I have attempted to give you that. In order to fully benefit from this book, I would like to ask that you first read chapter 12 (and do the principles outlined), then read chapters 1 through 11, and lastly read chapter 12 again. Reading chapter 12 at the beginning and at the end again will help you to accomplish the goals in life that you seek.

Chapter 1

A Worthwhile Journey

"Do not miss the purpose of this life, and do not wait for
circumstances to mold or change your fate."
Ella Wheeler Wilcox

"Go confidently in the direction of your dreams. Live
the life you have imagined."
Henry David Thoreau

"There are no speed limits on the road to excellence."
David Johnson

Writing a book is a challenging task for most, especially for
me since this is only my second time around. However, when you
write about something that you have experienced in your own life,
it makes it a joy and an easy process. This book is a compilation
of my personal experience while pursuing the Ph.D. degree as well
as things learned from other doctoral students and those who work
in academia. My inspiration for writing this book is twofold.
First, I went through the experience and know what it's like to
actually walk down that dreaded road towards the Ph.D. It can be
painful, making you want to give up. Others can benefit from the
mistakes that I've made along the way by not repeating them.
Secondly, this book grew out of the many workshops I've done
around the country on the subject matter. The workshop is called,

If you do the smart things now, you will complete the Ph.D. degree

"Strategic Planning for the First 18 Months of Your Doctoral Program." I have presented this workshop to undergraduate and graduate students in all types of colleges and universities across the country. I'm inspired to write this book because of the many students who have approached me at the conclusion of the workshop, requesting more of my time on an individual level and more information on the subject. I remember Cara, a student about to graduate with a master's degree and then enter a Ph.D. program, who approached me at the conclusion of a Salt Lake City workshop. She was extremely appreciative in that she learned from the workshop many of the crucial things that she needed to do ASAP before entering her doctoral studies. At the conclusion of a Washington D.C. workshop, a husband and wife—teary eyed (both graduate students) approached me and were extremely excited about the information that they learned. The husband said that he is now more motivated than ever before to complete all of the requirements and graduate. One of the most inspiring persons to date was a young man I met in Florida, named Steve (who was in his first year in a Ph.D. program). He approached me and shared that he felt lost and confused about what he should be doing. Unfortunately, Steve wasn't getting the information and direction that he needed from his advisors. But, after the workshop he said, "I now know what I have to do, and I'm more determined to do this and get it done." Individuals like these combined with my desire to make a difference are my inspiration to put this information in print so that it will be available to everyone who desires to succeed in a Ph.D. program.

Who Will Benefit

I believe that the content of what you will learn in this book will change your life, give you the tools to succeed, and inspire you to take action. This book was written for and is valuable for anyone who desires to succeed in graduate school. If you are contemplating returning to school, this book will offer vital information. If you are currently working on your bachelor's degree, this book will benefit you in preparing you and informing you about the process of graduate school and how to succeed. Those who are currently working on their master's degree will be many steps ahead as they consider the next level. Current Ph.D. students will find this book as a helpful road map through the journey. University professors, administrators, and advisors will find helpful information that will assist them in their preparation of students. Lastly, the information covered in this book will benefit someone who may not be involved in education but has a family member or friend who is pursuing a college degree. Knowing what to offer and how to help a friend has much value.

My Story

A day that's embedded in my mind forever is when I received an email from the vice president of the graduate school that read, "Congratulation Mr. Jones, I have just signed off on your dissertation and you are now Dr. Samuel Jones." Having the vice president sign off on my dissertation and send me that email was one of the most exciting days of my life, not to mention a huge relief. So in 2002, after 6 ½ years of hard work, making many mistakes, and correcting them along the way, I graduated with my Ph.D. degree in psychology from the School of Education.

Matriculating to earn a doctorate degree was not an easy task for me; many days I wanted to throw in the towel and return to a normal life. But there was something inside of me that would not allow me to quit. Taking classes, doing research, writing papers, networking, looking for financial assistance, getting married, having two children, and writing and defending a dissertation were a huge part of my life for those 6 ½ years. If it wasn't for my earlier years of literally reading at least 100 books on the subject of motivation, personal development, and attending workshops by some of the leading personal development coaches in the country, I would not have graduated. People such as John Maxwell, Zig Ziglar, Brian Tracey, Les Brown, Dennis Waitley, and Robert Schuler—just to name a few have made me into the person that I

If you do the smart things now, you will complete the Ph.D. degree

am today. I learned tools from those men that continue to impact my life and the lives of those around me.

My inspiration for writing this book is what I call a mild case of obsessive-compulsive disorder. I'm obsessed with helping others succeed. I have a tremendous desire to help others in making the decision to take the plunge into graduate school and ultimately to graduate in a timely manner with a Ph.D.

What You Will Get

A Chinese proverb says that "to learn the road ahead, ask those coming back." I'm sure you can agree with me that it makes no sense to try to re-invent the wheel or not to take advantage of, or receive coaching from others who have achieved what you desire. After going down that road already, I want to make it easier for those who will follow after me. The information you will learn in this book will make your academic and non- academic life comfortable and less stressful. I have added something at the bottom of each page that may be viewed as a motto, but to me it is a statement of truth, a guiding principle, and a constant reminder of what's necessary. That significant statement is ***"If you do the smart things now, you will complete the Ph.D. degree."*** One report that I read showed that only 49% of students who enter a Ph.D. program complete it and graduate. That's a shameful fact. More than 50% of entering Ph.D. students will drop out. I've also learned that those students who drop out for whatever reason are dropping out within the first 18 months or in the last stage which we call the dissertation stage. A good question to ask is, "WHY." Why are students dropping out in the first 18 months? Why are some not completing the dissertation? I can definitely relate. I've learned a great deal about the answer to these questions, and it is my hope that what you will learn in this book will be a source to lead you through your program and graduating.

If I Do The Smart Things Now, I'll Graduate

That's a fact! If you do the smart things, you will complete the Ph.D. degree. It's so simple, but yet so hard for many. Success in anything comes to those who have learned from others, who have prepared themselves for the task at hand, and who will take action. Most people have goals; unfortunately too many people make achieving a goal difficult. They actually bring difficulties upon themselves by being ill-prepared. Think about this. If an experienced carpenter set out to build a house without a blueprint, he may build it to completion but it will likely be a mess just waiting to happen. Earning a Ph.D. is like building your house. A house begins in one's mind. Then the mental picture is given to an architect. The architect will design and write out a blueprint, detailing every side, angle, and dimension of the house. Just like the architect, you must make a plan. *Your goal is to get the degree.* You need to have a plan in place on what you need to do step by step, and information that includes what to do when challenges occur.

If you do the smart things now, you will complete the degree. This book will assist you in what you need to do in the first 18 months in your doctoral program. Because if you do the smart things now, you will not make dumb mistakes, you will not be blindsided by things that can hinder you, and you will learn how to handle unexpected events even before they happen—and trust me, they will. So, I've included my very own statement of truth (if you do the smart things now, you will complete the Ph.D. degree) which is a motivating principle on the bottom of each page. This will help keep you mindful of what you are doing and where you want to go.

Upcoming Chapters

The succeeding chapters will provide you with some valuable information on getting that Ph.D. degree in your hot little hands. Chapter two asks the question, "Why pursue a Ph.D. degree?" It's good wisdom to gain insight into why you are doing something. The second chapter also gives valuable information on the benefits of having the degree. As you read along, I have attempted to make this book informational, motivational, practical, and interactive. There will be specific tasks (small and large) that you will be asked to do. **PLEASE DO THEM**. Too often we read something with an assignment to be carried out and we don't do it but instead will read on. THAT'S NOT GOOD! The information and assignments in this book are listed on purpose with an end goal in mind. So please carry the assignments out when you approach each. Secondly, at the end of each chapter is a blank single page with the heading "Hot Points." This page is for you to record notes from the reading, or to record any ideas that pop into your head that would be helpful. I used to have a bad habit of reading and not recording anything. My brain and your brain are limited in their capacity to retain and recall helpful information or hints. In the past, I would read a good book or go to a workshop, and great thoughts and ideas would come to my conscious mind, but I wouldn't write anything down. I just thought that I would remember it when I needed it. Very bad on my part. I've read hundreds of good books and have attended hundreds of seminars and workshops, and if I could go back and get all of the wonderful ideas that popped into my head while reading and listening, I would be the most informative and wisest on earth. But it's too late now; I'll just have to settle for being the second wisest! Trust me, as your read each chapter and carry out the assignments, you will have thoughts and ideas to pop into your head, so for your own benefit record them on the "Hot Point" page at the end of each chapter.

In my life I have learned the power of positive thinking. I have also learned the power of negative thinking. How we think will ultimately decide our fate. John Maxwell said that "unsuccessful people focus their thinking on survival, average people focus their thinking on maintenance, and successful people focus their thinking on progress." In chapter three, I will focus on established ways of thinking that can hinder your success in graduate school and ultimately your life. I call these established ways of thinking "Ph.D. Myths." A Ph.D. myth is something that many people have heard over and over again and now believe; fortunately, most of them are false. This chapter will help you to dispel these myths; because your thinking has to be right in order to succeed. The next chapter is a preparation plan prior to taking the leap into your Ph.D. program. It is not faith or wisdom to jump into something without preparing or jumping into something you know nothing about. To do that is a stupid thing and not a smart thing. The chapter will outline important things to do before taking the leap. However, if you are already in a Ph.D. program, then you will receive tools to help you avoid mistakes. The next four chapters will prepare you for the practical things you must do in the first 18 months in the program. Chapter nine will help you avoid the costly mistakes that graduate students make. I'm excited about what you will learn in chapter ten ("The Dreaded Dissertation"). In this chapter I will show you how to have written at least 30% of your dissertation before the end of your second year. In the final chapter you will learn the essential qualities that are necessary to be successful in your Ph.D. program.

How Can This Book Help You

Living in a fast-paced and busy society, most people, especially those in academia, seek to utilize their time to gain results. We don't have time to waste. For that reason, I have given 100% of myself in an attempt not to waste your time, and to be as practical as possible. There are at least four proven features that you will get from this reading. They are as follows:

1. A guide
2. Practical Exercises
3. Tools
4. Motivation

A Guide

A guide is a person who helps another reach a certain destination. Every person ever born requires some type of guidance. In specialized areas such as a Ph.D. program, it is extremely important that your guide has personal knowledge of the challenges in reaching your destination. The information in this book will give you specifics on what you should be doing, when to do it, and how to do it.

Tools

Tools are instruments that are used to get a job done. Imagine a carpenter without his tools. He has the knowledge and the blueprints to build a house, but he can't build without his tools. The information you will learn will be the instrument needed to reach your goal. When I am deciding or choosing a <u>how to</u> or <u>strategic planning</u> book to read, I always have two goals in front of me. One goal is that I tend to have a craving or desire to know something and I want that desire fulfilled, and the other goal involves using that information to help myself and others. You should approach this reading with similar goals.

Practical Exercises

As I mentioned before, action is needed to get things done. Practical exercises are located within the chapters. These exercises will help you to understand yourself, your goals, what you should be doing, and how to take action to get your Ph.D. completed. It's important that you do the exercises and not leave anything undone.

Motivation

Although knowledge and information are power, if you are not motivated or driven, then no matter how much you know, you will not complete your goal. Franklin Delano Roosevelt said "to reach a port, we must sail - sail, not tie at anchor – sail, not drift." In studying the subject of "motivation" for more than twenty years,

I have learned what works and what doesn't work. You will learn the art of using passion to get you to the finish line.

Let's begin with a simple exercise. Identify four desires that you hope to achieve from reading this book and list the benefit associated with each.

Desire: *(Example: I want to achieve motivation to succeed)*

Benefit: *(Example: It will help me to stay focused and determined*

Desire One:_____

Benefit _____

Desire Two:_____

Benefit:_____

Desire Three:_____

Benefit:_____

Desire Four:_____

Benefit:_____

Here is a wonderful story by Victor Hansen. If you internalize it and make it your own, you can expect great things to happen in your Ph.D. program, in your career, and in your life.

Action Leads to Success

Visualization is the most important foundation of success. You first have to figure out what it is that you truly want- love, respect, wealth, etc. Second, you have to believe that these things are already yours. See yourself as having that loving relationship. Visualize yourself being respected and admired by your peers. See yourself bringing home a million dollars a year.

Third, you must create a plan to bring these things into your life one action step at a time.

Wanting, desiring, wishing; these are all important parts of achieving your dreams. But participating in the realization of your dreams by taking action says, "Hey, I believe that what I want is possible so now I'm moving forward to get it!" You are showing that you have decided what you want and deserve, and that you have identified the action steps necessary in attaining your dreams and desires.

In the beginning, taking action may seem a little scary. You'll probably feel butterflies in your stomach when you take that first step. You may even think the fear will stop you at some point. But think of how you would feel if you never tried. If that doesn't convince you, close your eyes and imagine the overwhelming joy of seeing your dreams realized! There you are in your new home, or your fulfilling relationship, or getting that promotion!

Don't be surprised when fear shows up before you take action. Greet it with a smile and say, "Hello, I figured you'd probably be showing up." Then turn your back to it and take that step anyway. You will be rewarded for your decisive action.

Hot Points

Identify important information that you need to refer back to.

_____

_____

_____

_____

_____

_____

_____

_____

_____

If you do the smart things now, you will complete the Ph.D. degree

If you do the smart things now, you will complete the Ph.D. degree

Chapter 2

Why Pursue a Ph.D. Degree?

"I find the great thing in this world is, not so much where we stand, as in what direction we are moving."
Goethe

"Every evening, write down the six most important things that you must do the next day. Then while you sleep your subconscious will work on the best ways for you to accomplish them. Your next day will go much more smoothly."
Tommy Hopkins

Before answering the question of "why pursue a Ph.D.?," it is important that we first talk about what a Ph.D. is. I have learned over the years that it is better to ask questions and locate facts than to make assumptions. Assumptions are a fool's way of finding himself.

What is a Ph.D. ?

One of my greatest joys is teaching the "Introductory-to-Psychology" course to my freshmen students. These young minds tend to be quite inquisitive, but are not accustomed to finding or searching for answers as they relate to going beyond the first four years of college. To my surprise, I've learned that more than 90%

of my freshmen students do not know what the initials "P-h-D" stand for. Do you? Of course you do, but let's talk about it anyway. Well, it does not mean "Patiently Hoping for a Degree." Nor does it means "Pizza Hut Driver." The letters "P-h-D" means Doctorate of Philosophy. It carries two characteristics. First to earn a Ph.D. means that one has mastered a subject area (i.e., psychology, biology, etc.) and has extended his or her knowledge of that subject area through scientific studies and the writing of a dissertation. To earn the degree you will study everything or almost everything related to that chosen subject area that has been done over the years. You will become an "expert" in that specific area. Don't be thrown by the word "expert." An expert is a person who has a specialized skill or knowledge in some particular field. It does not mean you are the best in the field, nor does it mean that you know everything about everything. The Ph.D. is the highest academic degree available. The degree is extremely prestigious and greatly admired. People show respect to those who have a Ph.D. by calling them "Doctor." Less than 1% of the population has a Ph.D. You are about to become part of that elite 1%.

What is Graduate School?

The answer to this question may seem obvious, but to some it needs more explanation. Graduate school is the level of education beyond the bachelor's degree or four-year college. It is training in a specific area of research. It is for those who have arrived at some idea of what they want to do for a career. Research is a broad area that tends to include just about any thing that you can think of in the areas of business, education, medicine, social sciences, law, and so on. Graduate school gives you an opportunity to now find a specific area in a field to investigate, focus on, and learn about. Normally it takes between four to seven years to complete a doctorate degree depending on your area and the university's program requirements.

Graduate school in a Ph.D. program can be broken down into three stages. During the first stage, you do your course work. Also you learn the ropes; attend meetings and learn how to do research. Stage two primarily focuses on teaching; actual research, and completion of any qualifying exams or comps. In stage three you have completed your course work and all qualifying exams; you now work on your dissertation project and write it. You are what we call "ABD" (All But Dissertation).

RECAP

Stage 1……Learning the ropes, learning research, attending meetings

Stage 2……Teaching, doing research, completing qualifying exams

If you do the smart things now, you will complete the Ph.D. degree

Stage 3……Dissertation project and writing

From my personal experience, I have discovered that the first eighteen months and the dissertation stage of a Ph.D. program are the most difficult for most. In the first year, you are trying to find yourself, you are trying to learn what to do, and you are trying to find the right people to help you. This is my inspiration for writing this book.

Graduate school work is unique and very different from undergraduate school. In graduate school your work becomes practical and focused. You have an assignment now, and you will be required to develop it. Much of your time will be devoted to reading other scholars' work and developing your own agenda or area of interest. Also, your relationships with faculties, advisors, and other students will be closer and more intimate. Your success will depend on how well you work with significant people and your networking abilities.

Typically an institution of higher learning will be labeled "college" or "university." The title "university" usually indicates that the institution has a masters and/or doctorate program. A research-oriented university will offer doctoral programs. Many of the professors at research-oriented universities will be heavily involved in grant writing and research, often requiring doctoral students' assistance.

Not all departments at a university will offer doctorate degrees. Many students who desire to enter a university and earn a Ph.D. degree will think that the succession of degrees is as follows: "First I need to get my bachelor's degree, then my master's degree, then the Ph.D." This is not the case in every situation. You do not have to have a master's degree to enter a Ph.D. in many programs. Over 95% of my students are pleasantly surprised when they learn the truth. So remember:

You can complete your bachelor's degree and immediately enter a Ph.D. program.

However, there are some programs that require the completing of the masters degree first. You will need to communicate with your advisor to determine the requirements at your institution.

Why Earn the Degree

Why should I pursue a doctorate degree? The best person to answer this question would be you. However, I can offer my reasons to apply to a Ph.D. program years ago. I had three reasons that helped me to make my decision about pursuing this degree. First, I fell in love with psychology as an undergraduate and I wanted to gain a greater level of understanding human behavior and what made people tick. So, a Ph.D. degree appeared to be the source that I should go after. Second, I am passionate about helping people to succeed and win in their lives. I knew with an advanced degree that I would have a greater tool to help others. The Ph.D. would open the door for me to learn a great deal about human behavior, it would give me some practical tools to help others, and it would provide some authority to speak on the subject. Thirdly, I believed that I would enjoy being a college professor. There are many benefits associated with working in a college or university. We'll talk more about that later.

As you decide whether or not to pursue the Ph.D. degree, you can expect to get different advice from different people. The Ph.D. is primarily a research degree. It prepares you to teach and do research in a university setting. Also, it may lead to doing research work in industries, government agencies, and research laboratories. The degree also prepares you for management positions in organizations and to be administrators at colleges and universities. The Ph.D. degree will provide you with a strong theoretical and practical background in your chosen field.

Let's do something practical. View the list below and place a check by every field of work that sparks an interest in you.

Career Areas

Teaching   Music

Business (accounting, management, etc.)   Science

Working with Children   Computers

Medical (healthcare)

Working with the Elderly

Working with Adolescents

Physical Fitness

Art

Writing

Science (biology, chemistry)

Public Relations

Theater

Law

Engineering

Counseling

History

Math

Rehabilitation

Animals

Photographer

I'm sure that you checked off two or more items on this list that sparked your interest. There are some fields on this list or others that are not on this list that you undoubtedly feel passionate about. That's good. By the way, my list is not an exhaustive one. But here's the kicker; you can earn a Ph.D. in every area mentioned above and even others that are not listed.

Be that you are reading this book lets me know that you are not average. The average person and the person with no real goals would not take the time to read a book with a title that begins with the words "How to" or "Strategic Planning." You are not average; you are different. You are part of that 5% of our population that does not accept average, nor will you only strive to get a little. You want a lot and you focus on progress. This is worth repeating again: John Maxwell said that "unsuccessful people focus their thinking on survival, average people focus their thinking on maintenance, and successful people focus their thinking on progress." Here is a list of internal reasons to consider as to why you should go after a Ph.D.

Internal Reasons to Pursue the Degree

- **Achieving the greatest level of knowledge and information in your line of work**
- **Internal satisfaction or pride**
- **Being intrinsically motivated**
- **Having the potential for greatness**
- **Others are dependent upon your expertise**

Greatest level of knowledge

I believe that people are created to grow, learn, and to do their best. Although no one will ever know everything there is to know about any given subject, I believe we should strive to know everything that's possible to know. The Ph.D. degree affords one an opportunity to learn a great amount about some area of interest. There are numerous career fields that you can enter, and you should want to give your best.

Internal Satisfaction or Pride

Internal satisfaction is the feeling you have when you have achieved something great. Winning in life just feels good. An attitude of winning keeps you going; it gives you a reason to go after your goals. The day I walked across the stage to receive my diploma after almost seven years, I felt like I was on top of the world. I had just won the Heavyweight Championship of the world. I was "King" for a day. Internal satisfaction is not selfish pride or arrogance; it is a feeling of success. Earning the Ph.D. is worthy of your feeling some pride and satisfaction.

Intrinsic motivation

To be intrinsically motivated means that you are driven from within to succeed. You don't need or require money, fame, or others' approval to be driven. You are driven from inside yourself! There are some people that can not reach a level of satisfaction unless they pursue their goals. An internal need pushes them forward. This defines the Ph.D. student. This type of motivation is lasting because you stay motivated and you don't need some external reasons to go after important things in life.

Potential for Greatness

I believe that all people have the potential for greatness. However, most will never realize their potential. They allow situations, circumstances, and family backgrounds to stop them. You are unique! You brought something into this world that was not here before you came. To not give 100% effort to discover your greatness is the greatest of failures.

Others are Dependent on You

Your achievement in life is not only for you but for others. I believe that a purposeful life, one with real meaning, is one that lives to give to and help others. You need to see the earning of your Ph.D. as a means to give back to others. The knowledge that you will gain can make a difference in the lives of others. Don't you agree? Professionally, I view myself as a servant. I'm always sharing my knowledge and expertise with others.

Now that we have covered some internal reasons to strive for your doctorate, let's look at some external reasons.

Here are some (and not all) of the external reasons to obtain the Ph.D.

- Gaining a desired job or promotion
- Financial rewards
- Advancing society's knowledge in an area

Desired Job or Promotion

Your career choice and goals may require that you have a doctorate degree, especially if your goals are to teach or do research. If either is the case, then you will be externally driven to achieve the degree. Many people return to college for more training or to receive advancement in their careers. That is a perfectly good reason to go back to graduate school. With the very competitive society that we live in, it's becoming more and more necessary for advanced degrees. In years past, the four-year degree was an end to some means. However, today a four-year degree is nearly equivalent to a high school diploma. The opportunities to advance are more likely for those who have a higher degree.

Financial Rewards

There are financial rewards in earning the degree. The report below indicates the average level of income by degree earned in 2001 (Source: U.S. Department of Commerce).

High School Graduate	Some College	Associates Degree	Bachelor's Degree	Master's Degree	Professional Degree	**Ph.D. Degree**
$34,723	$41,045	$42,776	$55,929	$70,899	$100,000	**$86,965**

Let's face it; money is important. Your lifestyle and very existence require money to survive in this world. The quality of your children's education, the community you live in, and many things that you are able to do depend on your income. Need I say more?

If you do the smart things now, you will complete the Ph.D. degree

Advance Knowledge

Another external reason for you to pursue the Ph.D. degree is that we are the ones who through research help others in our society. For example, mentoring programs are on the rise throughout our nation. These programs are designed for those with knowledge and skills to help those with lesser knowledge or skills in an area. My dissertation was one that developed and evaluated the outcomes of an electronic mentoring (e-mail) program in which adults in the city served youths who lived in a rural area. I would like to think that my dissertation advanced society's knowledge on another approach to helping and serving others.

If I may add two more external rewards as to why you should pursue the Ph.D., they are (1) you get to hang a nice looking diploma on your wall, and (2) people will call you "doctor." Isn't that nice?

You Were Born to Win

Higher education in this country is available to everyone who is willing to work hard and is determined. Our lives were meant to be goal-directed and achievement-oriented. Les Brown said "we are born to win." I agree with Les that we are born to win. I teach a psychology course called "Life Span Development." In this course my students learn about the process of life from conception to death. Allow me to teach a little psychology here about life and death. The fact that you are born is an incredible phenomenon that medical science can not fully comprehend or explain. For example, _____ *(write your name on the line)* was conceived when his/her parents had sex, (Oops, let me use my more scientific terminology) was conceived when his/her parents copulated and your father released approximately one hundred million sperms (seeds). The sperm's journey towards the pathway to fertilize your mother's egg was unique. Your mother's ovaries are about eight to twelve inches away from the opening of her vagina. Considering the size of a sperm, that eight to twelve inch distance is equivalent to two miles! Over 80% of the sperm released die or don't travel the distance towards the egg. You are here now because you were determined, you worked hard, you out swam over 20 million others, and then, you successfully fertilized an egg. So as you can see, you truly were born to win from the beginning.

I'm not a fearful person, but the one fear that I used to harbor was not reaching my goals in life before I died. When one dies, it's too late. Recently, I was asked to speak at a friend's funeral. The friend died an untimely death. The service was to be held at the gravesite. As I drove onto the cemetery lot and parked my car, I couldn't help but notice the size of the area. That place was probably the largest cemetery in Alabama. As I walked across the area towards the location of the gravesite, I noticed the names, dates of birth, and dates of death on the plots of the deceased. As I continued to walk across the cemetery, thoughts of sadness intruded my mind. The sadness was not related to the people having died, but something else. It saddens me that in that cemetery, there are people who have died and have been buried, but who have not reached their full potential. And now, it's too late. I believe that that is the worst way for life to end. Cemeteries are sad because there is more untapped potential and too many unfulfilled dreams that will never be realized within those graves. Because of that we all miss out.

You were born to win, and you don't want to leave this earth without realizing your gifts. Les Brown once said that he wants to be used up when his time comes to die. He said that he wants to take nothing to his grave. This is why you should pursue the highest education available. Your life will have the opportunity to impact many. That's what a legacy is!

GOAL EXERCISE

If you are already in a Ph.D. program or plan to enter a program, list the degree that you will pursue and write out how the degree will help you and others.

Degree Area _____

How it will be helpful to you and others:

If you do the smart things now, you will complete the Ph.D. degree

_____

_____

_____

_____

_____

_____

_____

Now, as you work towards completing your degree, keep the above information at the forefront of your mind. One writer said, "Risk more than others think is safe. Care more than others think is wise. Dream more than others think is practical. Expect more than others think is possible."

Hot Points

Identify important information that you need to refer back to.

_____

_____

_____

_____

_____

_____

_____

If you do the smart things now, you will complete the Ph.D. degree

If you do the smart things now, you will complete the Ph.D. degree

Chapter 3

Myths About the Ph.D.

"Your life today is a result of your thinking yesterday.
Your life tomorrow will be determined by what you think today."

"Challenging popular thinking requires a willingness to be unpopular
and to go outside of the norm."
(John Maxwell)

What is a <u>myth</u>? If you look up the word in the dictionary, it would say that a <u>myth</u> is a legendary narrative that presents part of the beliefs of a people or explains a practice. It can also be an imaginary person or thing. Myths have been around since the beginning of man. There are myths about creation. There are myths about legends and great gods. There are even myths about graduate school and the Ph.D. degree. Knowing what's true and what's false is vital to your success as you think about entering graduate school or as you may already be in graduate school. A discussion of Ph.D. myths and what's true is relevant to impacting your thinking or to change some patterns of thinking that may already be established.

Why Discuss Ph.D. Myths

Myths are important to discuss because of the concept of repetition. Repetition is the mother of learning. That is, when you hear something over and over and over and over again, it's easy to begin to accept it as a truth or a fact, even if it's not true. The very definition of a myth is related to beliefs, and beliefs determine values and expectations. When we hear something over and over again and don't do research or challenge it, then it develops into our thinking and belief system. Ultimately, it impacts what we choose to attempt in life and not attempt.

Over the years, I have learned that there are established myths associated with graduate school and the Ph.D. degree. In fact, I accepted some of these established myths prior to my admittance into graduate school. A greater fact is that I delayed going to graduate school because I believed things I heard without investigating them for myself. If you intend to be successful in pursuing a Ph.D. degree, you need to understand fiction from facts; *your success depends on it.* Remember, thinking impacts behavior. Now let's examine what's not real and what is real.

Myth: *I don't have what it takes to be successful in a Ph.D. program.*

Truth: The Ph.D. degree is the highest degree offered. It takes focus, discipline, and hard work to succeed.

Several years ago, when I began my Ph.D. program, I thought that even though I was admitted into the program that I just didn't have what it would take to be successful. My thoughts were that I would engage in a futile exercise for a year or two, then, I would go back to being normal and quit this foolishness. Coming from a family of eight with no one ever achieving a bachelors or four-year degree, I thought to have earned my bachelors and master's degrees already were sufficient enough for a person of my background. My thinking was that my master's degree was the best that I could do. I thought only very intelligent people earn Ph.D.'s, and I'm definitely not one. Too many people have accepted the idea that they can only achieve educationally what is normal for the history of their family or only slightly higher. The truth is that if you are focused, disciplined, and will work hard, you will achieve your educational goals.

Myth: My undergraduate G.P.A. and my graduate school entrance exam scores are too low to succeed in graduate school and they are good predictors on how well I will perform in graduate school.

Truth: G.P.A. and entrance exam scores are not good predictors of how well one does in a Ph.D.

program. Primarily they are used to weed out the large number of students who apply for doctoral programs.

I'm sure as you prepare for graduate school, you will hear this lie often. I heard it quite a bit. I even believed it for a while. I spent many, many hours studying for the GRE. I paid over $200 to attend an eight-hour GRE prep course. If you had asked me how well I was going to do on the GRE, I would have said that my score was going to be a record setter. On the day of the exam, I was ready and full of confidence. After taking the exam, I had to wait about ten days to receive my score. When it arrived, my score was not one to be proud of. Although preparing yourself through prep courses and study guides are good things to do and you should do them, the final score is not a predictor on how well you will do in a Ph.D. program. True predictors of one's success can be better gauged in the program as it relates to staying focused, staying disciplined, and working hard.

If universities admitted every student who applied to Ph.D. programs, they believe that it would lessen the prestige and quality of their programs. Therefore, they determine that it is necessary to have some type of mechanism in place to assure the integrity of their programs. The truth is that past performance does not always measure future performance. If this myth were true, then different levels of school would be none existent; parents would find it a waste of time to train their children into maturity. Don't you accept this myth.

Myth: I'm too old to go back to school and succeed.

Truth: You are never too old to learn. The average age of doctoral students is 35. The average age of a black Ph.D. recipient in 2002 was 37.5. The average age of a white Ph.D. recipient in the same year was 33.9. Besides, the older you are, the more serious you may be about succeeding.

A hot button for me is when I hear people complain that they cannot do something or succeed because of their age or all of their responsibilities. I have read between the lines and have learned that the "too old" phenomenon really comprises fear, low self-esteem, and a lack of motivation. Too many won't even try because they are afraid of failure. It's a lack of self-esteem because the person does not feel confident in himself or herself to achieve and a lack of motivation to strive for better. Recently, I had a similar conversation with a forty-nine-year old married mother of two adult children. She explained that it would take her five years to earn her doctorate and that "at forty-nine I'm just too old." I responded by saying that in five years or sixty months you will be a young fifty-four and you have a choice to turn fifty-four with the degree or without it, which is best? DO NOT choose to allow your age to be an obstacle to your success. There are many who are sixty-five and older who have returned to graduate school and have earned their doctorate degrees. In 1992, while in my master's program at California State University, I met a wonderful and inspiring lady name Beatrice. She was sixty-four years old and was also pursuing her master's degree. This lady had been out of school for more than forty years and prior to entering school she had gone through an abusive marriage. She was excited to be back in school and was determined to succeed and graduate. We became close friends. She taught me how to go after my dreams, how to be determined, and how to stay focused in spite of challenges. Primarily, I learned from her just by observing her. She participated in on-and-off-campus events, and always made herself available to mentor and help others. Beatrice completed her master's degree in two years, joined toastmasters and went on to be an inspiring and motivational speaker, sharing her knowledge and experience in schools and organizations across the state of California. She was definitely a winner. Oh, by the way, did I mention that Beatrice was completely blind and used a guide dog to assist her around campus? WOW, what an inspiration for those who are mature in age and/or physically challenged!

Myth: Financial aid is only available for undergraduate students, and there are no monies available for graduate students and I would have to take out student loans, going deep into debt.

Truth: In many Ph.D. programs, you will choose a professor to work with, and this person will normally have some grant funds to pay your tuition and offer you a stipend (investigate this). Additionally, there is money available for graduate students through fellowships, scholarships, teaching and research assistantships, and special programs. You will have to do your research and network to find the money, because it is out there.

Years ago, when I was preparing to enter my doctoral program, I wrote over 200 companies and organizations requesting financial assistance in return for part time work or services. In my Ph.D. program and because of my efforts, I received a total of three different scholarships. Additionally, I earned tuition assistance and a stipend through teaching undergraduates. The money is out there; you just have to take the initiative and find it.

I am 100% totally, completely, and down right against taking out student loans. They can hinder you for years to come. Typically, most who graduate with their Ph.D. will have accumulated on average about $40,000 to $55,000 in student loans. The average loan balances are even higher for those who graduated with a professional degree, such as medical and law school. Those who have completed graduate school and have utilized student loans are very familiar with requesting deferments, forbearances, and struggling to pay them. Deferments and forbearances are two types of requests to delay paying payments on the loans due to

48

one's financial inability. The cost of interests on these loans over a term of twenty to thirty years is enormous. It's even higher when deferments and forbearances are included because when you delay in making your monthly payments due to financial struggles, interests and late fees will continue to pile up. Unless you land a high-paying job, you can expect to be making payments on your student loans when your kids enter college. AT ALL COSTS, AVOID STUDENT LOANS.

Another suggestion is at all cost, to avoid credit-card debt. Let's talk about the dreaded credit card. According to creditcard.com, in the 70's there were about 20 million credit cards circulated in the United States. Today, there are over 1.5 billion in circulation in the United States. With a population of about 295 million, that's about 5 credit cards for every citizen in the country. If you have a credit card balance of $5000 at 18% interest, it will take you twenty years to pay the balance off, provided you borrowed no more and made all your monthly payments on time. *That's frightening.*

One report I read found that the average graduate student carries six credit cards. The report indicated that graduate students accrued high credit card balances to help support them while in school. Trust me. I know because of experience that you don't want to graduate with your degree along with student loans and credit card baggage. One of the wisest decisions I've ever made was to *close*, *pay off* and *cutup* my four credit cards. I will never again be a slave to "Master Card" or try to find my way with "Discover Card."

"BUT WAIT" you may say. "I can't go to graduate school unless I borrow and go into debt. The financial aid office and the graduate school department advisor advised me to take out student loans. They said, "When you finish and graduate, you will make enough money to have made borrowing worth while, and your salary will be so high that you will pay off the student loans in a few short years." If you are thinking that way, then you are very normal, because you are thinking the way many graduate students think. It is true that earning a graduate degree places you in an above average income, but it is not true that your income will be so high that you can payoff a $50,000 student loan in a short while. The Federal Reserve reported that over 70% of graduate students with student loan balances of $40,000 and higher carried their loans on average to twenty years.

I am no different than most readers of this book. I too read books on financing graduate school, and they all advised the student to take out student loans. My financial aid department, academic advisor and others told me to borrow to finance my education. Unfortunately, I took their advice and have paid the price for the decision. I learned better as I began to work on my degree and even more when I completed the degree. I don't want you to make the same mistakes. I'm not in denial. I understand funding your graduate school education is a tough task. But, if you are willing to take the time to investigate, search, make some phone calls, talk to people, browse the Internet and fill out applications, you will find the money to finance your education. Here are 14 tips that will aid you in funding your education.

<u>Financial Sources:</u>

#1 Typically, if you have a good undergraduate GPA and your graduate school admission exam score is good, you will qualify in your program's department for tuition assistance.

#2 Find a professor in your program who is working on a grant doing research, connect with him and work on his project as an R.A. (Research Assistant). You can expect to work at least twenty hours weekly and receive tuition assistance and a monthly stipend.

#3 Talk with your advisor and check your department for any scholarships or fellowships. Usually, departments will have monies available.

#4 Check the graduate school department for monies or scholarships.

#5 Investigate the university campus wide for monies; talk to student affairs, academic affairs, and other departments. Make calls to departments, check their web sites, and talk to people in those departments.

#6 After your first year in the program, work as a GTA (Graduate Teaching Assistant). GTA's teach undergraduate courses and receive free tuition and a monthly stipend.

#7 Work part time on campus; look for these positions-- administrative internships, graduate traineeships, residence hall, counseling assistantships, reader or tutor position. Make sure you complete the Federal Application for Student Aid (FAFSA) so that you will be in the system if a work study position or other university-related aid becomes available.

#8 Seek scholarships and fellowships from funding references in your campus libraries, and from the Internet. Check Graduate School Funding Handbooks in book stores.

#9 Contact all of the following organizations below for scholarships (Beware: there are many organizations out there that offer assistance to help you locate scholarships, and free money for school; they are scams and they will bait you by guaranteeing to find you money for school provided that you send them an advance fee for their services. Avoid them because they are not legit; in the 90's I got suckered in and sent a check to them and only received a list of organizations to apply to. You can find those yourself on the web):

Check these out

College Fund/UNCF	www.uncf.org
e-scholars	www.studentjobs.gov/e-scholar.asp
Fast Web	www.fastweb.com
Gates Millennium Scholars	www.gmsp.org
Grants Net	www.grantsnet.org
Hispanic College Fund	www.Hispanicfund.org
Mellon Fellows	www.woodrow.org/mellon
Smart Student Guide to Financial Aid	www.finaid.org

#10 Ask parents to pay your way through school and offer them a service.

It is always best not to have an outside or regular job while in graduate school. But under the circumstances, you should do the following if the aforementioned efforts proved to be unsuccessful or not enough to cover your expenses:

#11   Get an off-campus, part-time job to cover your expenses, and attend graduate school full time.

#12   Get an off-campus, full-time job and attend graduate school part time.

#13 Contact the Federal Government and inquire about working in an inner city school or in an underserved community in exchange for tuition assistance while you attend graduate school part time.

#14 Contact your rich uncle and ask him to pay for your graduate school education.

Let me repeat, at all costs avoid student loans and credit card borrowing.

Myth: The work is too hard in a Ph.D. program.

Truth: The work is challenging, but not too hard to the point that you will not succeed. When you apply the right tools and you are determined to succeed, YOU WILL.

This is important, and I say it is a myth because at this point in your academic career you are working on your unique interests and what you love, unlike undergraduate in which you were taking those grueling multiple choice exams and writing those papers on topics that you hated that were assigned to you by your undergraduate professor. However, in your Ph.D. program, primarily you will be matriculating towards what is intrinsically inspiring to you and brings you total satisfaction. When you consider what's inspiring to you, your Ph.D. work becomes a joy and not a chore. Avoid the naysayer; working towards the Ph.D. is exciting and enjoyable.

Myth: It takes too long to complete a Ph.D. program.

Truth: The average time to complete a Ph.D. program is just 4 ½ years. The actual range is between 3 to 7 years, with most completing the degree between 4 to 5 years.

Some programs may be longer; however, the average is just 4 ½ years. The only thing that needs to be said here is that this small amount of time and commitment to your future is a small price to pay for the eternal rewards. Don't you agree?

Myth: I won't enjoy life, and I won't have a life while in a Ph.D. program. My entire existence will be working and studying all day long.

Truth: Not so. It is important that you balance your Ph.D. program with doing other things unrelated to school.

Recently on a bright and sunny Saturday afternoon, I was doing the family laundry and playing with my two-year-old son. My daughter came into the play room and informed me that she heard a loud bumping sound coming from the laundry room. I rushed to the laundry room and noticed the noise was coming from the washing machine. I lifted the lid and observed that all of the clothes had shifted to one side, causing an imbalance resulting in the bumping sound. Does this sound familiar? I realigned the clothes by spreading them evenly around the agitator. After that, the washer was fine. Life is like that washing machine. If we place all of our time and work into improving one area of our lives, we experience an imbalance, leading to unhealthiness and eventually breakdown. The Ph.D. work is important, and it does require good quality and an appropriate quantity of your time. However, it is vitally important that you live a balanced life. If we consider the Ph.D. as the academic or mental part of your development, then it is vital to add social activities, physical activities, and spiritual activities in order to live a balanced life and stay healthy so that you won't experience bumps in your life. Remember the P-H-D is not an acronym for "Permanent Head Damage," or "Potential Heavy Drinker," or "Probably Headed for a Divorce." It is a testament that you have taken on a major project and have completed it and are deserving of the rewards associated with it.

Having other non-academic things in your life will actually help you academically. You need family time, exercise time, play time, vacations, and relaxation times and time doing absolutely nothing. Do these important things because your mind and body require time when there is no pressure, no mental challenges, and no deadlines to meet. Having a balanced life will reenergize you to perform at a higher level.

Myth: No one in my family has ever achieved a doctorate degree. Therefore, it's unlikely that I could ever achieve it. I guess it just runs in the blood.

Truth: Today and in the future to come, individuals all over the U.S. are going on to earn doctorate degrees in spite of their family history. You do not have to accept the error in thinking that your family or background are pivotal in your own success.

What's true about this myth is that many people have accepted this line of thinking and will not even attempt to succeed in areas of their lives. They have placed what I called "blood lined self imposed ceilings" on their lives. In other words, no one in my family has ever done that before; therefore, I can't either. Thereby, educationally and financially they only achieve a slightly better life than their parents. This is more wrong thinking than a myth, but it's an unfortunate reality. It is the very reason why in our society we see a family line of doctors, lawyers, top executives, or entrepreneurs. And in others, we see a family line of those who never earned a graduate or professional degree, or a line of workers who remain at the bottom.

I have eight siblings, seven from my blood line and one adopted by my parents. Out of a family of ten, I'm the only one to earn a degree beyond the bachelors. (Only one other has earned a bachelor's degree.) I decided to make a better life for myself in the area of education and helping people. In fact I have a bachelor's, three masters, and a Ph.D. degree. Your family background does not have to determine your success. Use your family line as a motivational vehicle to succeed.

Myth: The dissertation is an unbearable task, and I will never finish it.

Truth: The dissertation doesn't have to be an unbearable task if you start off on the right path. The final chapter in this book will help you to defeat what I call "disserphobia."

The dissertation to the Ph.D. student is the bar exam to the law student. It is a task that culminates your graduate school experience. It brings together in an organized fashion what you have been doing the past years. If you start off on the right foot, the dissertation *Will Not* be an unbearable task; it will be an enjoyable task as it was meant to be. Too many students get to this point and never complete the dissertation and never graduate. Chapter 10 will provide you with good insight on how to make this process winnable.

Myth: A professor's life is not exciting (for those who may be considering this field).

Truth: Not true, there are many exciting things about being a college professor. Hear Ye! Hear Ye! Here are some of the exciting benefits of being a college professor.

- Flexible work schedule
- Opportunities to do research on what interests you
- Opportunities to get grants to fund major projects
- Traveling to other locations and doing research with others researchers
- Presenting workshops in your area of specialty
- Teaching students
- Expanding what you know into areas that you are not familiar with
- Impacting generations to come with your work
- Good pay with multiple opportunities to increase

The above-listed benefits are by no means an exhaustive list. Being a professor becomes part of one's life, and every professor with whom I have communicated has said that he or she absolutely loves what he or she is doing and couldn't imagine doing anything else.

Again, it can not be emphasized enough that your thinking along the lines of what is a myth and what is true is essential to your success. How you think and what you believe affect what you attempt in life. So, I have tried to remove any false thinking that may have been established over the years.

Identify and list four established negative thoughts that you have regarding your entrance or pursuit of a graduate degree.

1. _____

2. _____

3. _____

4. _____

Reread and high-light sections of the chapter that are similar to your beliefs and locate other readings (via the internet, books, etc.) that challenge these negative thinking patterns. On the sections below, identify the new way of thinking that challenges the negative thinking(s) mentioned above.

1. _____

2. _____

3. _____

4. _____

Recommended Readings:

Possibility Thinking (Dr. Robert Schuler)

Thinking to Change (John Maxwell)

If you do the smart things now, you will complete the Ph.D. degree

Hot Points

Identify important information that you need to refer back to.

_____

_____

_____

_____

_____

_____

_____

_____

If you do the smart things now, you will complete the Ph.D. degree

Chapter 4

Things to Do Before Starting

"You have to do your own growing no matter how
tall your grandfather was."
Abraham Lincoln

"Your limitations and success will be based, most often,
on your own expectations for your self. What the mind
dwells upon, the body acts upon."
Denis Waitley

It is my hope that chapter three proved to be new revelation and inspiration for you to move beyond myths or any erroneous thinking and pursue what you are capable of achieving.

One of my favorite psychologists is Dr. Abraham Maslow. He came up with the idea of "self-actualization" – maximizing your ability in areas of your life. It means to reach your full potential or to bring out your peak. He formulized that to become a self- actualized person, an individual must have achieved certain levels of success in his or her life in other areas. His theory is referred to as a hierarchy of needs in which specific areas of life must be achieved or met before moving to the next level. See illustration below:

Being Needs

Self-actualization

Esteem Needs

Belonging Needs

Safety Needs

Physiological Needs

Deficit Needs

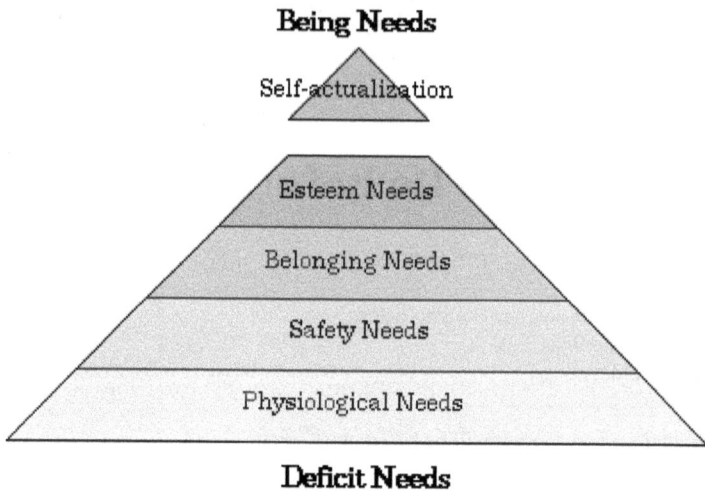

There are different types of needs that are essential for one to become self-actualized or an achieving person. First are the physiological needs (i.e., food, water, oxygen, sex). These needs are necessary to sustain or keep life going. The second level of needs is related to your safety and security. That is, having a home to live in, in a safe environment. Levels three and four both deal with relationships and belonging needs. We need to be loved and have good relationships with other people in order to develop a healthy self esteem. With a healthy self esteem, you feel confident and prepared to take on any challenge. When all these needs are in place, it enables you to achieve your goals and to reach the peaks in life.

Just like it's important to progress through these stages, equally important is to have certain needs in place before starting

If you do the smart things now, you will complete the Ph.D. degree

your Ph.D. work. Your success depends on being prepared. That may include putting some preventive measures in place. I have identified eight relevant needs that should be met prior to pursuing your doctorate degree. They are as follows:

1) Work or Intern
2) Be Passionate about the Field
3) Contact Department Professors
4) Learn from Current Students
5) Have Definite Goals
6) Have family Support
7) Have no major Crises going on
8) Know your Strengths and Weaknesses

Some of these may not apply to you, but they are all good information to have. If these things are done beforehand, your journey is going to be a sure success.

Work or Intern in Field

Pursuing your doctorate degree in any field will be a major part of your life. In fact it's almost like having a baby. Adding a new baby to your family is life-changing. Babies are demanding, time-consuming, and costly. Well, going to graduate school is demanding, time-consuming, and costly. It places new demands on you and is time consuming. Since you have decided to make this type of investment in your life, it's worthwhile to spend time interning (or volunteering) or working in the field that you are about to pursue. It is time-consuming to do this, but I don't think it is necessary to spend years working in the field before starting graduate school. Most people will be able to determine whether or not this is the line of work for them in a matter of months. For example, if you desire to pursue a Ph.D. in biology or math and your goal is to teach, then you should intern or do some volunteer teaching or tutoring for students. This will help to give you a firm foundation and to determine if that is what you really want to do.

My purpose for pursuing the Ph.D. degree was to enter academia as a professor. Before starting the Ph.D. program I worked as an adjunct instructor at a community college and at a local university. Having the master's degree I met the minimum qualification to work in those settings. While teaching in those institutions, I began to connect with new professors as well as those professors who had been in the business for many years. I learned what academia and research was all about through my association with them. Within my first semester of teaching as an adjunct professor, I knew that this was to be my life calling.

Identify in order of priority three career fields that interest you:

1. _____

2. _____

3. _____

For each of the three fields write down the educational
requirements and any work experience needed

1. _____

   _____

   _____

2. _____

   _____

   _____

3. _____

   _____

   _____

If you do the smart things now, you will complete the Ph.D. degree

Now that you have identified three areas that interest you and educational requirements, next, you want to think about your preparedness for the task at hand.

Passionate about the Field

If I were forced to choose between being an intensely motivated person or an intensely passionate person, hands down, I would choose the latter. Passion deals with very strong feelings (love, hate), and motivation deals with a motive or a reason to do, have or be. Although both are necessary, motivation tends to fluctuate with what's going on around us. However, to be intensely passionate about something is more internal and long lasting. The feeling of passion is so strong that many people would give their life for the cause. Passion can cause you to HATE a situation in your life so much that you are compelled to do whatever it takes to make a change. For example, I knew of a man who was maxed out in debt in his life and he was living pay check to pay check. His eight credit cards were maxed out, his car payment made him sick, and his mortgage payments and student loans were overbearing. He hated his circumstances. This man had such strong feelings about making a change that he sold his house and moved into a cheap apartment on the poorer side of town. He cut up and closed out all of his credit cards, vowing never to use credit again. He sold his nice, new car and paid cash for a cheaper car. He worked four jobs and completely gave up his

If you do the smart things now, you will complete the Ph.D. degree

social life. In less than nine months he was completely debt-free. And, in less than four years he paid cash for a new home and is living better now than he has ever before. That's *Passion* with a capital "P."

It is necessary that you have the same type of intense feeling about what you are about to study. You must love it! You must be willing to do whatever it takes to succeed. Passion means that it's easy for you to turn off the television so that you can do quality work on the research paper. Passion means that you can easily say no to unimportant demands of your time from others. Passion means it is easy for you to stay up late and get up early to do your studies. If you decide to pursue a Ph.D. in micro-biology or computer science and the subject matter doesn't burn inside of you with passion, then you may be investing your time in the wrong area. Find an area that you love and commit to giving it 110%.

Contact Professors in the Department

Would you buy a $500 pair of shoes without trying them on first? Of course not. This is a major difference between undergraduate and graduate school. It is not really necessary that you, as an undergraduate student, speak with your future college professors about their research and interests before deciding to join the department. However, as a future or current graduate student, you want to contact the department's professors to learn about their research and other areas that may interest them. This will help you to determine if your area of interest and goals are in line with what's going on in the department. Not too long ago my wife entered graduate school to work on a master's degree in the university's biology department. Her specific interests were related to anatomy and physiology. Before entering the program she investigated and learned that none of the biology professors in the department had an interest or a research agenda that matched her plans. Therefore, she sought out another department with professors whose research agenda closely matched her goals. She joined the biology department, but is doing her research with another professor outside of the department.

It is absolutely necessary that you contact the department professors to learn what's going on. This will help you to find where you will fit into their program.

Identify three areas of research in which you hold a strong interest (i.e., working with autistic children, computer software programs, etc.):

_____

_____

Learn from Students

Students who are matriculating in a department are the best people from which to learn information about the department. They know the department well. They have first- hand knowledge on how helpful or non-helpful the people are within the department. I suggest that you see two types of students in the department. You want to meet those who are *new* (completed at least three semesters) in the department and those who are in the midst of writing their dissertation. Getting the new students' and dissertation writers' perspective about a program is invaluable. However, one needs to be mindful of what I call the whining student. This person focuses on finding things wrong with everything and is always complaining. Stay away from this person. Remember your rationale for communicating with other students is to get general knowledge about the program and the people, and not to get involved with someone's personal problems.

Here is a list of questions to ask the new students:

Questions for New Students
1) Why did you choose this particular department?
2) How helpful is the staff?
3) Do you meet regularly with your major advisor; how helpful is that person?
4) How are you progressing in the program?

5) What setbacks have you experienced?

6) If you could change something, what would it be?

Here is a list of questions to ask the senior students, those who are in the dissertation stage of their program:

Questions for Senior Students

1) How long did it take you to get to this point in your program?

2) How did you choose your dissertation topic?

3) How helpful is your dissertation committee?

4) Have you experienced any setbacks in writing your dissertation?

5) When did you start writing your dissertation, and when do you expect to graduate?

Remember, your rationale for communicating with students is to gain some general knowledge about the department and the key people. This information could mean the difference between your deciding to join this department and program or not. You want to find a good fit. You will learn quite a bit from talking with students. However, let me add that I believe my personal individual progression and success is not contingent upon whether or not other students are succeeding. You should adapt that mindset too. It will help you along the way.

Definite Goals

Having goals for your education is one thing, but to have _definite_ goals for your education is something else. Definite goals are more defined, precise and specific. It's acceptable to have undefined and unclear goals related to your education and career while working on an undergraduate degree. Unfortunately, too many students enter graduate school with little to no idea of what they want to do. They want the graduate degree, but they don't know why, or what it is they want to study. Prior to entering a Ph.D. program you need to KNOW what your goals are. Knowing your goals and having some idea of what your interests are will help speed up the process of your developing your own research agenda. You need to KNOW what you intend to do after earning your doctorate degree.

From my research of those who enter Ph.D. programs, I learned how doctoral students develop their interests and career choice. Here is a list of some of the information that I've learned from that research from questioning Ph.D. students:

- Goal developed out of having worked in several different lines of work after which a life calling or destiny was developed, which led to a return to college.

- Goal developed out of a new passion for a specific area.

If you do the smart things now, you will complete the Ph.D. degree

- Goal developed out of an interest that has been in one's heart for years or decades.

- Goal developed out of current line of work and desire to advance and/or to become an expert in the field.

- Goal developed out of desire to be more competitive in business or in education.

- Goal developed out of a desire to know more about something.

- Goal was to become a university professor, for which the Ph.D. is required.

The above is just an abbreviated list of reasons as to how some students came to enter a Ph.D. program. Your own definite goal to enter a Ph.D. program may be something other than those listed. But you need to know and be able to communicate what your goal is. My primary goal for entering a doctoral program was a love for teaching and helping others. Think about your reasons because it is crucial that you know exactly what it is you want to achieve. Having this issue settled before starting your Ph.D. work will keep you focused and on track. Goals are important, but even more important are these two questions: Do you know how to set a goal, and do you stick to the goal until it is achieved? First, let's understand something. A goal is something that is set to be achieved at a future date. That was simply enough, wasn't it? Most people do not have goals for their lives. They approach life with whatever happens will happen. As a Ph.D. student you will learn or be *forced* to learn or fail if you *do not learn* to set goals and stay with them until completion.

Goal setting starts when we apply for graduate school. Here are some goals to be achieved by the student:

- *Investigating different graduate schools programs*

- *Ordering transcripts and records from undergraduate school*

- *Completing the application packages and all of the important forms*

- *Scheduling and taking the graduate school entrance exam*

- *Obtaining letters of recommendation*

- *Scheduling course work*

- *Choosing an advisor*

- *Having clear objectives and goals when meeting with advisor*

- *Process goals throughout the program*

- *Dissertation goals*

If you do the smart things now, you will complete the Ph.D. degree

So as you can see, goal setting will be a part of your life throughout your graduate school experience and beyond. Let's go back for a minute and learn how to set goals. Goals must be something that are achievable. For most of us, the goal of becoming a millionaire in two years is not achievable. Achievable goals are exactly what is implied: "achievable or obtainable. This means with effort and a specified time period you can do it. You should have short-term goals (achievable within 12 months) and long-term goals (achievable in 2 to 5 years). Your mind and body need to be goal-oriented. You can train yourself to be a goal-oriented person. Here are some short-range goal ideas. On a regular basis I like to create those "to do" lists. I make out a simple list of things I plan to get done. My list may include cleaning out the garage, balancing the weekly budget, contacting three university departments inside of five days to inquire about presenting my workshop, or completing ten pages in a week for an upcoming book.

Long-term goals are important, but they must be measurable. For example, it is feasible for a student with a newly earned Ph.D. degree to have a $100,000 annual income in five years as university professor because the average income of a professor is about $60,000 (higher in some fields); however, it will require some planning and work. To build one's income from $60,000 to $100,000, you will have to learn about and take action in the areas of furthering your research agenda, acquiring grants, publishing, developing workshops, and doing speaking engagements. As you progress in those areas you will see measurable increases in dollars coming in towards your goal.

Do this exercise now:

Write down 15 things to do that can be achieved in 30 days and do them.

Goal	Completed On
1. _____	_____
2. _____	_____
3. _____	_____
4. _____	_____
5. _____	_____
6. _____	_____
7. _____	_____

If you do the smart things now, you will complete the Ph.D. degree

8. _____   _____

9. _____   _____

10._____   _____

11._____   _____

12._____   _____

13._____   _____

14._____   _____

15._____   _____

Doing this exercise is a good practice to prepare you for doctoral studies. It will train your mind and body to carry out goals to completion. At the end of the 30 days, examine how many of the items you completed, and if all were not completed, then ask and search yourself to determine why those items did not get done. For the incomplete items, ask yourself these questions: What obstacle(s) stood in the way of my completing that goal? What could I have done to remove those obstacle(s)? How motivated

If you do the smart things now, you will complete the Ph.D. degree

was I to complete that goal? If I were to make that item a goal again, what would I do differently? Answering these questions on the incomplete goals will expand your thinking and teach you how to evaluate your actions. So go for it!

Family Support

You are about to invest four to seven years of your life into graduate studies. You can expect things to change in your life. Family conditions, finances, social relationships, and other activities that you normally engage in will change. Change is inevitable. Our world is evolving and changing all the time. Even the computer that you are using today will be outdated in three to five years. Entering graduate school to work towards the Ph.D. will impact your life and those who are a part of your life. If you do not handle change properly, you will not succeed. I never knew how much I needed my wife's support until I entered graduate school. In fact, I know that I would not have completed my doctorate degree without her. She was there to keep me going; she inspired me during the challenging times. She kept me on track. Whether you are married, single and dating or unattached, have parents, siblings, relatives or close friends, having support is rewarding during your graduate school years.

While in graduate school, typically your work status will change. Your friends and associates will be earning an income and you may be absent from the work force for a period, whereby, you may experience a change in your lifestyle as it relates to money. Your relationships with friends will change; in that a great deal of your time will be spent doing your course work and research. You won't have as much time to socialize or respond with a "yes" to participate in too many extra-curricular activities. How you handle these changes can hurt you or help you. Here's a suggestion on how to handle those relationships. Go to those who are closest to you and explain to them that you are entering graduate school and that you need their support because you have a habit of getting sidetracked. Ask them to hold you accountable by contacting you on a regular basis to keep you on track. That way, they will understand that you are busy and that they are contributing to your success.

My wife Angela (we call her Angel, and she certainly is one) was extremely supportive during my graduate school years. She handled the bulk of our household expenses through her job; and she allowed me to dedicate quality time to my school work at the expense of not spending time with her. During my dissertation phase, I would spend hours upon hours looking for information in the library and writing. In fact, it was normal for me to come to bed at 1 a.m. or later. Talk to those who are close to you to make sure that they are on your side.

Here's an assessment exercise for those important people:

Go to your spouse (or significant other) and three of your closest contacts and ask them the following question and rate each individual:

Question

Would you be very supportive, supportive, or not supportive in my going to graduate school to work towards a Ph.D. degree in _____ (state area)___ so that I can do work in or get a job in _____ (state career choice)_____ which will include my spending large amounts of time studying?

Name	Very Supportive	Supportive	Not Supportive
Spouse (or significant other)			
Friend #1			
Friend #2			

You can expect most people to be very supportive. The information that you will learn from their responses is a good indicator of who will be there for you during difficult times, and their commitment to sacrifice some of your time which will be dedicated to your graduate school work.

If you do the smart things now, you will complete the Ph.D. degree

Major Crises

I've included information in this chapter that explains what you should do and what needs to be in place before you start your Ph.D. work because I want your course for success to be set. Most of us know of people or family members who started a major project in the midst of a crisis going on in their lives. That's not good. Do not start a Ph.D. program while going through a divorce, experiencing major financial problems, physical illness or under some type of mental stress. These things can hinder your success. The Greek philosopher Aristotle once said "that the unexamined life is not worth living." Nothing can be more frustrating than starting your graduate school work and not consider everything that's going on in your life. I know that something is always going on in life, but you need to be certain that you have matters under control and that you are stress free. If I've seen it once, I've seen it a thousand times; people jump into graduate school in the midst of a major crisis. The end result is not being able to give attention to the work. Therefore, failure, disappointment, and a quick exit tend to follow. So examine your life to make sure you are crises-free.

There is a cost when starting a Ph.D. program. Answer these questions as if you are about to start graduate school:

1. Is my spouse 100% in agreement with me starting a Ph.D. program?

2. How will entering graduate school full time affect our income?

3. Am I involved with lots of extra curricular activities that may hinder my success in graduate school?

4. Who will be impacted if I quick the extra curricular activities and how will it affect our relationship?

5. Am I willing to give up some things to work on my Ph.D. degree?

6. Am I ready to commit four to seven years to graduate school?

7. Why do I want to earn a Ph.D. degree?

8. What will I lose if I go to graduate school, and am I okay with losing it?

9. What will I gain by going to graduate school?

The purpose of those questions is to make you think. You need to think about what you are about to get yourself into. Although some of your answers to those questions may be answers that you don't like or may be negative, don't fret: Remember Benjamin Franklin, who was a scientist, an inventor, a statesman, a printer, a philosopher, a musician, an economist, and one of our founding fathers. As you can see, he was a brilliant man. He had a very interesting way in which he made important decisions in his life. Franklin's way of making decisions was to list the two options and identify and tally up the positives of both options. Whichever option had the most positives, that's what he went with. I actually used this method many years ago in my life to help me make a very important decision. At the age of nineteen, I was contemplating leaving my hometown, Alabama, and make a move out west to California—the Land of Opportunity. I took a piece of paper and wrote Alabama on one side and California on the other side. It looked like this:

(List of Positives)	(List of Positives)
If I Stay In Alabama	*If I Move To California*
1. remain closer to family	1. more school choice
2. keep current job	2. more things to see
3.	3. newer opportunities
4.	4. land of opportunities
5.	5.
6.	6.
7.	7.
8.	8.

When I carried out this decision-making procedure, I came up with about four positives for staying in Alabama and over 20 positives for moving to California. So I moved. Most people, when faced with a similar decision, will make the decision by counting up the pros (positives) and cons (negatives) of a decision. Counting up

If you do the smart things now, you will complete the Ph.D. degree

the positives is best, because the high number of positives in something is what really successful people focus on. When billionaire real estate developer Donald Trump looks at a depressed property, he does not focus on the negatives, but rather his focus is on the positives of the property and its potential. He once said, "Since you have to think anyway, you might as well think big." Do this exercise. List all the positives of the decision not to go forward to earn your Ph.D. and list all of the positives of going on to earn your Ph.D.

(List of Positives) *Not Going to Graduate School*	(List of Positives) *Going To Graduate School*
1.	1.
2.	2.
3.	3.
4.	4.
5.	5.
6.	6.
7.	7.
8.	8.
9.	9.
10.	10.

My guess is that you have more positives for going than for not going; am I right?

If you do the smart things now, you will complete the Ph.D. degree

Strengths and Weaknesses

I am not the best speller in the world. I'm not even the best speller in Birmingham, Alabama where I live. Everything I write I have my chief editor (the wife) to review it for me. She is excellent at the English language, it's her strength. I'm encouraging her to enter one of those national spelling bee competitions. Spelling is not one of my strengths. Thank God for my computer's Spell Check. It took many years but now I have a pretty good idea of what my strengths are.

As you are about to enter your Ph.D. program (or you may already be in a program), you should know what your strengths and weaknesses are. In graduate school you will have to work extremely hard on your weak areas as they may be related to your specific program. On the other hand, take your strengths and tailor them to your program. For example, you are not a good writer, and writing is a major requirement in your Ph.D. program; however, you are excellent at doing research. In this case, take extra writing courses and practice the skill of writing until you become efficient at it. Since you are good at doing research, gear your Ph.D. towards doing research (taking more research courses and presenting your findings). Here are five readily available sources to gain some insight into your strengths and weaknesses.

#1 Your graduate school entrance exam (GRE, MAT, GMAT, etc.) score

If you do the smart things now, you will complete the Ph.D. degree

Depending on which you took, there may be sections that include writing, math, and statistics each with a singular score. You can access your score to determine what areas you are strong in and what areas you are weak in.

#2 Your undergraduate transcripts

Review your undergraduate transcripts. How well did you perform in the area of math? How well did you perform in English or writing courses? How well did you perform in analytical courses? How well did you perform in specific areas that are related to your graduate school major? Reviewing your grades in courses taken over the four to five years in undergraduate will help to identify where you are.

#3 Prerequisite areas

Prerequisites are courses that are at the beginning level of a similar more advance course or knowledge/information that is needed to take on the next level up. For example, if you have never used a computer before, then it will be necessary to take a beginning computer course to learn the basics before advancing into more advance programs. Therefore, gaining knowledge of the course requirements in your Ph.D. program will help to assess what you need beforehand.

#4 Undergraduate College Professors

If you do the smart things now, you will complete the Ph.D. degree

Most Ph.D. programs require as part of the application package for the student candidate to have three letters of recommendations with a least two from your previous professors. Typically, most professors will give a good to excellent rating of you. And sometimes they are not always candid and honest. Go to your undergraduate professors, those who know your class performance best, and ask them to share with you personally and honestly what they see as your strengths and weaknesses. Also, get their opinions on how you can improve in those weak areas and how you can maximize your areas of strengths.

#5 Others

All of us have contacts with others who know something about our abilities. Go to them. Ask them for their opinion regarding your strengths and weaknesses. You will be surprised at how well others have observed you over the years. My wife and others who are close to me have shared areas of my development with me that I had no idea existed.

Remember, you are making a commitment for your future success. You want to get started on the right footing. The next four to seven years of Ph.D. work may be the most challenging assignment that you will ever experience. If you make sure that the aforementioned eight items are in place before starting this new venture, you will stay focused and succeed.

If you do the smart things now, you will complete the Ph.D. degree

Hot Points

Identify importation information that you need to refer back to.

_____

_____

_____

_____

_____

_____

_____

_____

If you do the smart things now, you will complete the Ph.D. degree

Chapter 5

Your First Year in the Ph.D. Program

"What the mind of man can conceive and believe,
the mind of man can achieve."
Napoleon Hill

"If you want confidence, act as if you already have it.
Try the "as if" technique."
William James

WOW, you have been accepted into the Ph.D. program at the University of Whatever. CONGRATULATIONS! Your G.P.A., Entrance Exam Score, and application proved worthy enough to get you in. So what do you do now? Don't worry; you will choose or be assigned an advisor, and your department will give you guidance. This chapter is designed to be informational as well as practical. You will learn what to do and be encouraged to do specific tasks. Not all university programs are the same. Variations exist to program specifics. Therefore, some items in this chapter may not apply to your specific Ph.D. program.

I have through personal experience and research identified eight very important tasks that Ph.D. students should do in their first twelve months. These eight tasks are not all inclusive; you need to carry out other program duties as well. Let's get started.

If you do the smart things now, you will complete the Ph.D. degree

Departmental Handbook

Years ago in California, I applied for a job and was hired to be a restaurant manager. My first week on the job did not include working in the location at all. My assignments for the first two weeks were to read through three, eight-inch-thick manuals. These manuals were quite exhaustive; I learned everything that I needed to know about that specific restaurant business. At the completion of training and reading those manuals, I had to take a written test that made sure I understood the restaurant business. Your Ph.D. program's department will have a departmental handbook. This handbook is important, and it consists of information that you need to know as soon as possible about your program and the department. This book will include the following types of information:

1. Program requirements to graduate
2. Course description information
3. Rules and policies of the department
4. Guidelines and normal practices of students
5. Staff information
6. Important dates and time lines
7. Funding information
8. Professor information and research agenda

Ooops, I've been taking it for granted that you know what a research agenda is. Just in case you don't, let me explain. University professors were once where you are now. No man or woman came out of their mother's womb as professors. They all started out the same. Just like you, they went through undergraduate school, and traveled through the rigorous process of getting admitted into a Ph.D. program. A research agenda is an area of interests to which one studies and adds new knowledge. For example, your major may be computer technology. This field is changing all the time; so your research agenda may be to do lab work in computer technology to learn more and advance what you know.

Get the department handbook now and read it cover to cover. Get to know the department's staff and learn their functions in the department. This will help you down the road. Also, you want to meet and get to know the faculties and their research agendas. Do the assignment below and check off items as they are completed:

Assignment	**Completed on**
Get the Department Handbook	Date got it _____
Read it cover to cover	Date completed it _____

Any questions from your reading   Date got answers _____

Write down important information that you learned from the departmental handbook that you need to be kept apprised of:

_____

_____

_____

_____

_____

_____

_____

I've learned that many Ph.D. students are unaware that there is a departmental handbook for their majors, and I've also learned that many of those who are aware of the book may have it in hand, but will not read it; they find out important information that's in the book much later and oftentimes too late — a costly mistake. Do the above assignment NOW!

Develop an Annual Calendar

Organization is an important quality that Ph.D. students must have. An annual calendar is a helpful tool in staying organized and not missing important meetings, assignments, and deadlines. I used one of the large desk calendars that you can buy from Wal-Mart for about $2.00. When I was a student, I would take the department calendar and review all information in it that needed my attention or attendance (i.e., department meetings, guest speaker events, presentations, out of town conferences, etc.), and then I would list that information on my desk calendar. The calendar is always a work in progress, because you are always adding new and upcoming information to it. Additionally, include non-academic information on it. This calendar should be hung on the wall in a place in your home that you see everyday.

Some information that you list on your calendar can be classified as important, and other information will be considered urgent. Important information on your calendar would be events or dates that are relevant and require some attention but won't cause a heart attack. Then there is the urgent information on your calendar. This information is highly significant and demands your attention and could cause harm if not handled in a timely manner.

I recommend that you use a colored pen or a colored highlighter to note urgent information on your wall calendar. Go to Wal-Mart, buy the wall calendar, list important information and dates on the calendar, and hang it on a wall that you will see daily.

Although I have mentioned Wal-Mart several times, trust me; I received no commission for items sold at the store. But as graduate students we all learn the importance of being thrifty in our spending.

Apply for Financial Assistance

Applying for financial assistance is something that you should do before entering the Ph.D. program and afterwards. Some assistance requires that you be enrolled into the program before applying. Search your major department for in-house assistance; search for assistance on the university level; and search for assistance outside the university. Do some networking on campus to find the right people who can direct you in the way of funds. Also, your library will have numerous scholarship manuals for your usage. To be successful at getting financial assistance, you have to be determined and persistent, and to look everywhere for it. Refer to chapter three for sources that I've identified.

Complete a Program of Study Form (PSF)

The PSF is simply a schedule of all the classes that you intend to take over the course of your program. It should list each semester or quarter of each year with the average time to complete a Ph.D. being 4 ½ years. So you are writing out your four-to-five-year plan. Doing this early keeps you organized and on track. Complete this form with your major advisor, and be sure to have him or her to sign it. Although you will complete the form for the extent of your program, it is flexible, meaning you can go back and make changes on it as you progress or your interests change. Keep a signed copy of the PSF in your filing system and utilize it at each registration period. Two major benefits of this form are to keep you *organized* and on *track*. You will know what courses to enroll in each semester and you will stay on track in meeting your graduation goal.

Transfer Related Master Credit Hours

There were many exciting times in my Ph.D. program, but I have to admit, one of the most exciting times was when I discovered that a 500 level, three-credit-hour child development course that I took in my master's degree program was equivalent to or satisfied the 600 level child development course that I had listed on my program of study form in my Ph.D. program. I completed the equivalent course form, got the right signatures, and needless to say I did not have to take the 600 level child development course.

98

If you have a master's degree already, after completing your program of study form for your Ph.D., review it with your advisor to see if you can eliminate repeating a similar course in your doctoral program. Most programs allow up to six hours to be substituted if you've earned a grade of "B" or better from your master's program (sometimes bachelors). Every little bit helps, and this may shave some time off completing your Ph.D. degree. To make this process simple, take your master's degree transcripts and your completed Ph.D. Program of Study form and list the names of the courses, including course number, that appear to be similar or have similar descriptions below:

Master Level Courses   Ph.D. Level Courses

1. _____   1. _____

2. _____   2. _____

3. _____   3. _____

4. _____   4. _____

5. _____   5. _____

6. _____   6. _____

If you do the smart things now, you will complete the Ph.D. degree

Now that you have completed this, share it with your advisor and explain why you believe that the master's level course is similar to the doctoral level course. To be effective in making your case, you will need to attain the description of each course from the catalogue of your master's program, or the syllabus for that course, or a statement from the professor who taught that course. Getting and presenting all three sources should be your plan of action. Do this your first year.

Apply for Assistantships

Typically there are two different types of assistantships. One type is a Research Assistant (R.A.). An R.A. usually works ten to twenty hours per week with a professor assisting the professor with his research. Professors in your department may have grants and are involved in some research related to the grant. Get to know these professors who have these grants and evaluate whether or not the grant is related to your area of interest; if so, then speak with the professor about joining his team as an RA. You should consider joining the team even if the research is unrelated to your area. You want the experience. Typically the compensation for an assistantship is tuition assistance and/or a stipend.

Another type of assistantship is a Graduate Teaching Assistant (GTA). The GTA teaches undergraduate courses in his/her area under the supervision of a professor. For example,

100

you are working towards a Ph.D. degree in biology. You will develop lesson plans and teach freshmen level students in introductory biology. See chapter nine on common mistakes that beginning teachers make. To find these types of assistantships, speak with your department chair and your major professors and look for postings. Also, important to note is that you may do a GTA or an RA outside of your major department. In my psychology program I had a concentration in Human Development. Fortunately, my university had a full Human Development Department in which I had been taking courses and becoming very familiar with professors in the department and their research. Because of my relationships with the Human Development Department, I worked for two years as an RA with one of the professors in the department. So you have more than one choice. For the GTA position, the amount of income you will earn from it depends on the number of hours worked or the number of classes taught or the amount of funds available.

Normally you would select to do only one of these, an RA or the GTA. If you select to do a GTA, I strongly recommend that you apply for it your first year and begin teaching during your second year. Teaching inside of your first year is too early because it requires lots of prep work and time. And because you are a first year Ph.D. student, your focus should be on becoming familiar with your program and learning the ropes and not teaching classes. Under normal circumstances it's okay to begin working as a research assistant at any time. The experience you'll gain as an RA is good, and it is not as taxing as teaching. So go for it!

Professional Journals

Professional journals contain literature reviews and/or scientific studies found within most disciplines. They consist of articles and research written by scholars who were excellent enough to get their work published, not an easy task, as you will learn. Communicate with your major professors and the senior graduate students for the best scholarly journals in your field. Becoming familiar with and reading studies early in your program will give you a heads up on what other scholars are doing and what published work looks like. After reviewing several journals in your field, you will begin to notice the type of research that really interests you. Do not order a subscription to these journals because they are very costly, with some priced at more than $500 annually. Use your campus library copy.

Start your Dissertation

YES, start your dissertation work now. Dissertation is not a project that you want to begin after completing everything else. It should start in your first year in the program (see chapter ten for specifics).

Choose an Advisor

Your advisor without a doubt will be the most significant person at the university to you. Most programs will allow Ph.D. students to choose their own advisor. Others will assign one to you. This person can be a blessing or a curse. The advisor that I had was from Hell. Literally Speaking. This man made my life a living hell. I believe that Satan sent him in my path to destroy me. From his perspective and only his, everything that I did was awful. He was a destroyer of students and not a helper. I would say that 95% of my ideas from his perspective were terrible. He was difficult to communicate with and overbearing. Our relationship was so bad that I even contemplated leaving the university. Believe me; you don't want to make the mistake that I made in selecting an advisor. This person can make you or break you. The next two chapters will provide you with what you need to know about advisors and how to select the right person for you.

Survival Tips for the First Year

In addition to following the steps above, it's important that you be mindful of other things related to your body and health. To strengthen you for the academic journey, here is my list of tips (that are not academically related) that you may want to include in your life.

- Eat a healthy diet (green vegetables, fruit, meats high in protein), and avoid eating too many sweets and fatty foods.

- Join a gym or use the on-campus facilities and exercise regularly (Your student fees are covering the cost, so you might as well use your on-campus gym facilities).

- Do some non-academic reading for enjoyment.

- Live an organized life; plan your activities for the next day and week.

- Spend some time enjoying friends and family.

- Make some new friendships outside of the university.

- Stay positive.

- Learn or take on some new hobbies.

Staying involved in non-academic activities will help you keep your sanity. So live a well balanced life.

If you do the smart things now, you will complete the Ph.D. degree

Hot Points

Identify important information that you need to refer back to.

_____

_____

_____

_____

_____

_____

_____

_____

If you do the smart things now, you will complete the Ph.D. degree

Chapter 6

What to look for in an Advisor

"Failure is an opinion. It is either an educational
tool for starting over or an excuse breeding tool
for saying it's over."
Doug Firebaugh

"Know the true value of time; snatch, seize, and enjoy
every moment of it. No idleness, no delay, no
procrastination; never put off till tomorrow what you
can do today."
Earl of Chesterfield

"Dare to live the life you have dreamed for yourself.
Go forward and make your dreams come true."
Ralph Waldo Emerson

In this chapter you will learn a great deal about the advisor
and how to get the most out of the relationship. This is a very
important person to your success. The advisor can make you or
break you. I have experienced very negative and very positive
guidance from different advisors. Because the subject of advisors
is a significant factor in your success, making the wisest decision
in choosing the right person and benefiting from the experience is
important. First we will look at the role of the advisor and then
the qualities of a good advisor.

If you do the smart things now, you will complete the Ph.D. degree

The Role of the Advisor

An advisor is one who advises and gives directions. You are matriculating towards the highest degree that universities offer. Therefore, at this junction your relationship with an advisor should be very different than your relationship with your advisor when you were a freshman in college. There are expectations of the advisee; you should know basic information, and you should be self-directed and mature. Those are qualities that most first-time freshmen lack. I've learned through experience that the role of the advisor in doctoral programs should be determined between the advisor and advisee. You must take an active part in deciding what's best for you. Every Ph.D. program and department are different, so your program may vary from what you will learn here. The normal functions of an advisor include the following:

- o Assist you with the development of your program of study.
- o Assist you with program requirements and make sure that you are taking the correct courses.
- o Work with you on research projects.
- o Be available to answer your questions.
- o Assist you in developing your dissertation committee.
- o Provide new information to you as it develops.
- o Be a mentor.
- o Monitor your progress.

Holistically speaking, I view the advisor as a map. This person assists you to getting from point A to point B, and provides you information about what's along the path and what to look for down the road. There is a huge difference between advisors in undergraduate school compared to graduate school. In undergraduate school, there is a distance between you and your professor. In graduate school and research, you and your advisor will work side-by-side and are considered somewhat equals, unlike undergraduate where the power line and role assignments are understood between student and advisor. In research and graduate school, you will both learn from each other. Both of you will come up with ideas, and you will make discoveries together.

If you do the smart things now, you will complete the Ph.D. degree

110

UNIVERSITY OF ALABAMA
Fall Commencement
December 16th, 2002

If you do the smart things now, you will complete the Ph.D. degree

Qualities of a Good Advisor

As I mentioned before this person is crucial to your success. I have experience bad and good advisors in my own journey. In fact, I wouldn't be where I am today without the assistance of a man named Dr. Rex Culp. He is a model of what a good advisor should be. He was very instrumental in my success. He made himself available whenever I needed him. He included me in his research projects and taught me some basic research skills that I needed. I have identified thirteen qualities that you need to look for in an advisor, and under each quality, I have placed a strategy to help you determine if the potential advisor has that quality.

#1 Personable and Approachable

This person needs to be personable and approachable, that is to say, someone who is a people's person and with whom you feel comfortable and can get along well. You should be able to talk freely and easily with this person. You should even like this person. Early in my Ph.D. program I did not take the initiative in selecting my own advisor; therefore, the department assigned one to me without my doing an investigation of this person. Needless to say this person was sent from Hell by Satan to torture me. He was not personable and approachable. When visiting his office, I always felt tense and uncomfortable. Don't let this happen to you. Be involved in selecting a person and make sure you like him or her.

How do I determine if the professor is Personable and Approachable?

Strategy

You simply learn this by visiting the individual(s) several times. Schedule some appointments with the individual(s). Stop by their offices sometimes unscheduled. In your conversations and interactions you will be able to detect whether or not the person is approachable and personable.

#2 Patience Enough to Bear with you Without Complaint

I believe that patience is a quality that most people lack. In our computer age and busy world, some people do not take the time to consider how their actions may affect others. Then there are those who do not care how their actions affect others. Trying to work with an impatient person who has authority over you is awful. An impatient person can be overly demanding, inconsiderate of the necessity of allowing you an appropriate amount of time to complete something, and will only think Rush, Rush, Rush, and more Rush. Because you are a new Ph.D. student who will make mistakes along the way, you must have someone who will help you and will be understanding. We all need some guidance, and the impatient advisor has forgotten that he/she was once in your shoes.

How do I determine if the person is patient?

Strategy

From my experience with this, you will need to do some detective work. Communicating with other students is the best approach (see chapter 7). Also, you can detect patience by taking a class from the professor. Through taking a class you will be able to determine how well this person works with students and level of patience. Try to assess the professor by getting the answers to these questions:

1) *When presented with a problem, conflict, or difficult situation, how does the professor respond?*
2) *When presented with deadlines, how does the professor respond?*

#3 Never feels Threatened by your Capabilities

Some Ph.D. students are extremely sharp. They may be more knowledgeable than their advisors. If this is the case, a good advisor would want to help make you even sharper and would not feel threatened. A good advisor will give you credit and extra inspiration where you excel.

How do I determine if this person feels Threatened?

Strategy

Investigate and find the answers to these four questions:
1) *Is the person one who often praises and compliments students' work?*

2) *If the person has several student publishings, are any students found as the first author?*
3) *Does the person attempt to dominate or monopolize others who work with him?*
4) *Does the person(s) share his/her resources with others?*

If, through your investigation, you answered "NO" to one or more of the questions above, then this may be a person who feels threatened by others. Avoid him or her like the plague.

#4 Someone who can MOTIVATE you to action

Nothing is more dull than an advisor who is not a motivator or an enthusiast. Motivation is a quality that one has that propels another to move forward in spite of roadblocks. While you are meeting potential advisors, you will be able to determine in a matter of minutes those who are exciting and motivating and those who are not. My advisor Dr. Rex Culp was an incredible motivator. Every visit to his office was a wonderful experience. He would always greet his students with exciting persona and was always encouraging. I remember during one of my most depressing situations in my program, I met him with a decision to quit the Ph.D. program and to do something else. I just became overwhelmed with some of the people that I was working with who were not supportive and were against all of my efforts. His belief in my abilities and his encouraging words actually made me feel like I was born again. I felt like a new person who could accomplish anything. I left his office that day with a new outlook and was more determined than ever to succeed. You need a motivator and a person who encourages you.

How do I determine a Motivator?

Strategy

This is easy to determine. A motivator and encourager is a positive-thinking person. No matter what negative event or situation comes his or her way, he or she will always respond with the potential possibilities in it and will always look on the bright side of bad situations. In talking with a potential advisor, you want to share some setback experience you had, and without asking for advice, just wait—watch—and—see; a motivator and encourager will seek something positive in it or encourage you and a non- motivator will throw a pity party with you.

#5 It's Helpful if this person has some familiarity with your area of Interests

Although it's not a major factor, it is usually good if your advisor has some knowledge of the specific area in which you are interested in pursuing. In other words, your advisor may be a tenure-psychology professor whose research agenda focuses on adolescent development, but you are a student in the psychology department, and your interest is in the area of sensation and perception. These are two entirely different agendas and receiving research guidance from the advisor will be limited. However, this

116

is only a small factor and should not be a biggie in whom you choose.

How do I determine if the potential advisor has similar interests?

<u>**Strategy**</u>

Well, you can share what you are interested in with the potential advisors and inquire about their knowledge or interest in that area. Also, you may want to review any published work by those professors to see if their interests are similar to yours.

#6 Good Time Management skills and organized

Having good time management and organization skills is important and should matter to you. I remember visiting one of my professor's offices to discuss a course. It was the most horrific environment that I have ever seen. There was no organization, and he was not aware of my scheduled visit with him because he couldn't find his schedule. Piles of papers were scattered on his desk and floor. Books on his shelves were not organized. It was a total mess. Although this particular professor was a respected and an outstanding scholar, I could not trust him in assisting me while his own life was out of order.

How do I Determine if this person has good time management and is organized?

<u>**Strategy**</u>

Find out if this person keeps his appointments. Does he start his classes on time? Is he late with returning information or graded papers to students? View his office and observe for cleanliness, organization, structure, and whether he is student friendly.

#7 Student-Oriented

This quality may sound like the first quality of personable and approachable because to be student-oriented, the advisor must be personable and approachable. However, the difference is that to be student-oriented includes characteristics associated with being what I call "Student Like." That is to say that the person hasn't forgotten what it's like to be a graduate student. This person is familiar with and still appears to be connected with students' concerns and happenings.

How do I determine student-oriented?

Strategy

I determined this in the past through three means. First, in my interactions with professors, I tend to be able to see how interested the person is with students by how interested the person is in me and how I'm doing. I've learned that good advisors want to know you, your family, how you're progressing in the program and your plans after graduation. An unconnected professor is one who is strictly business. Second, find out if the professor attends students' research presentations. Third, find out how other students view the professor.

#8 Defends you when you are not around

There is an abundance of politicking in doctoral programs. Because of the competition for funds, resources, and assignments, bickering may occur in some relationships. Not often, but sometimes you may come across persons who put you down in their conversations with others to help make themselves look good. Isn't that horrible? But in some circles it exists. A good advisor will defend you and look out for your best interests.

How do I determine if this person will defend me?

Strategy

You learn this again by doing your investigative work with the advisor's current and past advisees. A good rule of thumb is, whether this person contacts you, providing you advance information that you need to know so that nothing catches you on the blindside.

#9 Works well with other students, faculty members, staff personnel and administrators

You definitely want an advisor who is well rounded and has a good working relationship campus wide. Lots of benefits are gained when your advisor has a good reputation with the university.

During one of my most difficult challenges in graduate school, my advisor did all that he was able to do to help me and then he referred me to one of the university's administrators for more help. Going to the administrator on behalf of and the reputation of my advisor proved to be beneficial. I was able to get exactly what I needed. The administrator had great respect for the advisor which made my job quite easy. Also, when your advisor has good working relations with the university, he tends to have more resources available for you. So look for someone who has a good rep and good working relations on campus.

How do I find out if my advisor has good working relations?

Strategy

This is easy. I'm sure there are other ways to learn whether or not a potential advisor has good working relationships with others; however, I found the best way to learn this information is to make personal visits to administrators, deans of schools, department chairs, and office personnel (i.e, secretaries, office managers, etc.). Ask these individuals whom they would suggest as a good advisor and why. By asking those individuals that question, you will learn how well known the potential advisor is, as well as why that person may be a good advisor for you.

120

#10 Provides honest feedback about your strengths and weaknesses

I have never met the "Perfect Ph.D. Student." The truth is, there isn't one! You need an advisor who will be honest with you about your strengths and areas that need improvement. It will affect other areas if you don't know what your strengths and weaknesses are. If your doctoral program requires lots of writing and you don't write well, you need some critical and honest feedback on weak writing areas, as well as information on how to improve it. Also, you need your advisor to take notice of your strengths and to help you utilize them to your advantage. If you are one who has a difficult time receiving constructive criticism or your feelings are hurt easily, then you should not pursue a Ph.D. degree, because criticism is coming your way. Go to your advisor after the relationship has been established and ask for feedback on what he or she perceives as your strengths and weaknesses.

How do I determine if my advisor will give me information on my strengths and weaknesses?

Strategy

You can learn this from other students and through your own working relationship with the advisor.

#11 Involves you in his/her research

Although involving you in their work is not a determining factor on whether or not this makes for a good advisor, it is an excellent benefit. I believe it's important that your advisor connects with you in his or her research for at least two reasons. First, this is the person whom you will more than likely see more often for advice, and working with this person will enhance your skills in doing research. Remember the Ph.D. is a research degree. Second, when you graduate and start your job search, this person will have first-hand knowledge about your capabilities and could write you stronger recommendation letters due to the personal experience in working with you.

How do I determine if this person will involve me in his/her research?

Strategy

The best way is to investigate two areas. First, simply go to the advisor and inquire about being a part of his or her research. Second, ask around to see if this person normally has students working with him on projects.

#12 Assistance with Organizing your Dissertation Committee

You should want your advisor to help you organize your dissertation committee. This committee usually consists of about five individuals, and your advisor will have very good insight on who could better assist you in serving on the committee. Your advisor will have been working with you over the years while in the program, and this person better understands you, your interests, and your capabilities.

How do I determine if an advisor would be helpful?

Strategy

See #9 above.

#13 Helps you to graduate in a reasonable time

One of your primary goals when you enter a Ph.D. program is to complete it, walk across that stage and receive your diploma. Am I Right? You do not want to make attending graduate school a lifelong career. Nor do you want to become ABD (all but dissertation) and never graduate. When I started my Ph.D. program, I couldn't get my mind off the day in the future on which I would receive the award. Some 50% of students who enter a Ph.D. program never graduate. YOUR ADVISOR IS CRUCIAL IN YOUR GRADUATING IN A REASONABLE TIME!!!!!!!!!!!!!!!!!!!!!!!!!!!!!!!!!!!!!!!

How do I determine if the person has this quality?

Strategy

Go directly to potential advisors and inquire about how long they think an individual should be in the program and then graduate. Also, inquire with other students who are currently being advised by this person to see how far along they are progressing towards graduation.

These are some of the qualities that I have found to be necessary as you go about looking for the right person who will impact your number of years in the program. Use these listed strategies to discover whether or not the individuals have those qualities. I'm sure there are other strategies that can be used to determine the qualities of the potential advisor, but these have worked for me and others.

Type of Advisors

Now that you know the role of the advisor and qualities to look for, let's examine the two types of advisors: tenured and non-tenured professors. It is important to note that in some programs an advisor may not be a professor. I have knowledge of people in administrator roles serving as advisor to students. However, most advisors will be professors.

There tends to be some characteristics connected with the two types of advisors mentioned. Here is what I've learned as it relates to the two types:

Tenured Professor
Has less time available for advises.
Is more experienced.

Has a larger caseload of advisees; therefore you have more advisees to compete with for time.

Have more resources and monies available.

Travels more.

Is more stable at the university.

Knows how the game is played.

Knows other faculty members in department and outside of department to help you succeed.

Non-Tenured Professor

Is more availability.

Has more pressure.

Is less experienced.

Has a smaller caseload of advisees; therefore you have fewer advisees to compete with for time.

Works hard to become tenured.

Travels less.

Has less money for research.

Is less stable, may seek other opportunities.

May be more dedicated to your success.

Knows fewer faculty members in the department and outside of the department.

Those are the characteristics I've learned that tend to be associated with tenured and non-tenured professors. However, important to note is that the above list is not exhaustive and may not apply to every tenured and non-tenured professor. **Also, it's important to note that I am in no way suggesting nor implying that one type of advisor mentioned above is better than the other**. That is something that you will determine as you use the suggested ideas in this book.

Let's do a self-assessment exercise. The purpose of this self-assessment is to simply take another look at things that you already know about yourself. It's helpful to first look at yourself again before choosing someone to serve as your advisor. Place a check under each column number that fits your personality. The 4 indicates the trait is "very strongly" like you, a 3 indicates "strongly like you," a 2 indicates "somewhat like you," and the 1 indicates "not much like you."

Trait	4	3	2	1
I am a self starter, and I don't need anyone to push me.				
I set goals and time lines for myself.				
I know what it is that I want, and I have ideas on how to get it.				
I am self motivated, and I don't require another person to motivate me.				
Others have accused me of being a high achiever.				
I am energetic and focused.				
I have a positive outlook, and I'm an optimistic person.				
When I fail, I see it as an opportunity and not a set back.				
I am a risk taker.				
Typically I work hard, am determined, and never give up.				

Now total your score. A score of 34 to 40 means that you thrive on success; you are a person who expects to succeed, and with a small amount of direction from an advisor, you will succeed. A score of 27 to 33 means that you too can succeed, but you require more time with an advisor. Also, you need an advisor who will give you

If you do the smart things now, you will complete the Ph.D. degree

a little push. A score of 26 or less indicates that you need lots of direction, and you will require an advisor who will help you to stay motivated throughout your program. Try to match yourself up with an advisor who can help you achieve your objectives based upon this self assessment. If you know you need a motivator, then find that person. If you are a self starter and disciplined, you don't necessarily require someone to stay on top of you.

Remember, the advisor is someone who should help you, involve you in his or her research, keep you informed of important information, look out for your best interest, and help you to graduate in a reasonable time.

Hot Points

Identify important information that you need to refer back to.

_____

_____

_____

_____

_____

_____

_____

_____

_____

If you do the smart things now, you will complete the Ph.D. degree

Chapter 7

Choosing an Advisor

"Consult not your fears but your hopes and your dreams.
Think not about your frustrations, but about your unfulfilled
potential. Concern yourself not with what you tried and failed
in, but with what it is still possible for you to do."
Pope John XXIII

"Whatever you are, be a good one."
Abraham Lincoln

In this chapter we will be discussing one of the most
important decisions you will make in your academic career,
choosing an advisor. This person can make you or break you. The
reason this person is so important is because he plays a key role in
guiding, directing, informing and insuring your success.
Therefore, this major decision must be handled as if your life
depended on it. Proven techniques in choosing the right person are
incredibly important.

Thinking about my own experience; I did not follow
through, and I allowed my major department to choose an advisor
for me. Bad! Bad! Bad! To this day, I regret allowing that to
happen. This person made my life miserable. He was more of a
hindrance and an obstacle than a helper. The worst part about

132

working with this person was that he also was on my dissertation committee and provided ongoing obstacles that delayed my completing the degree. You don't need someone (who is not a good team player), no matter how talented, to be a part of your team.

After working with this difficult person for more than two years, I made a smart decision to make a change. I did my homework and came up with eight functions to carry out in selecting the right person for me. If you do these things, you can almost guarantee your success in choosing the right person for you. These eight functions are meant to be done in order as they are listed. Again, let me remind you that every program is different. Some programs may assign an advisor to you, and you may or may not have the option to change, which is extremely rare. Also, depending on the program, you may have the option to select someone outside of your area. Answers to all of these questions should be in your departmental handbook, which I'm sure you have already read. As you go through this investigating and selection process, remember the qualities of a good advisor that are laid out for you in chapter 6.

#1 Pin-point several

You need to identify those individuals who serve as advisors at your university and in your major department. You can find this out by visiting them and inquiring whether or not they function in that capacity. It would be helpful to you to identify more than three potential advisors. As you are meeting these individuals, and most will probably be professors in your department or program, you should think of yourself as an employer who is interviewing potential employees who will work in your company in the customer service department. When I think of meeting and selecting advisors, "interviewing" comes to my mind. I am trying to determine who's the best person for the job in working with customers. Therefore, pin point several so that you will have a choice. Don't stress over this; if you make a bad choice, you should have the right to make a change.

Go ahead and list the names of those who are potential advisors. Actually, at this point just about every person is a potential advisor. We will go through the elimination process as we move along further in this chapter.

Name   Title

1. *(Sample John H. Smith)*   *(Assistant Professor)*

2. _____   _____

3. _____   _____

4. _____   _____

134

5. _____   _____

6. _____   _____

7. _____   _____

8. _____   _____

9. _____   _____

10._____   _____

11._____   _____

12._____   _____

Now that you have listed the names of the prospects (use additional sheets if necessary), you can began your investigative work.

#2 Find out when and attend their research groups meetings
If the candidates that you selected are professors and they have research meetings, then you want to obtain permission to attend one or more of their meetings. Typically these meetings consist of the professor and his/her team of graduate students working on

their projects. Attending these meetings will give you an opportunity to observe how the professors interact with students and the type of projects that the professors are currently working on. This gives you the advantage in seeing the persons in action.

#3 Read their research work

Since the advisors are likely to be professors in the department, knowing their research work is good information because these are the same individuals whom you will ask later to serve on your dissertation committee. Through reading their work you are learning at least three things about the individuals:

1) what their interests are
2) whether their interests are similar to yours
3) whether the person(s) background is a right fit for your dissertation committee down the road

Since you have now identified potential advisors in step #1, list their name and research agenda or interests:

Name
Research Agenda/Interests

1. *(Sample: John H. Smith)*   *(body composition & nicotine)*

2. _____   _____

3. _____   _____

4. _____   _____

5. _____   _____

6. _____   _____

7. _____   _____

8. _____   _____

9. _____   _____

10._____   _____

11._____   _____

12._____   _____

Now you have a good working list of the potential advisors and their area of research. Look these over and try to see how you may fit into an area.

#4 Give the prospect a copy of your work and ask for feedback
At first thought, you may ask these questions: What if they are too busy to read my work? Why should they help me now and I'm not even their advisee, nor am I a student in their class? Don't fret! From experience, I've learned that most professors are honored and appreciative that new students in the department would request their brilliance in examining a piece of their work. At this point you really don't care what their thoughts are on the paper, but rather, the value in this for you is an opportunity to see how the person will interact and communicate with you. I know of a situation in which a student gave her advisor a paper, requesting his feedback. When the two of them met to discuss the paper, this particular professor lost control and yelled, "WHAT IS THIS? YOUR PAPER IS A BUNCH OF SCRAP; YOU CALL YOURSELF A GRADUATE STUDENT! YOU SHOULDN'T BE IN THIS PROGRAM!!!!" That student was devastated to say the least, and after that she never showed him another paper to review again. However, your strategy as you prospect is totally unrelated to the quality of the paper; you want to see how the person interacts. If the paper is a bad paper, you want to be treated with respect and politeness, and receive constructive feedback.

138

This will give you an opportunity to see how the person may be in the future.

#5 Drop by their offices and ask questions (unscheduled)

University professors are busy people. So why I am suggesting that you drop by their office without an appointment? A few years ago, I was doing a workshop in Miami, Florida, on this very topic. My audience consisted of graduate students, university professors and administrators, and event coordinators. In the workshop, I said, "You should visit potential advisors in their offices, unannounced and unscheduled." And WOW, the response from one administrator was not nice. The administrator said that "students should not go to their professors' office without a scheduled meeting." I politely asked why. The administrator said that "professors are very busy people and under a lot of pressure; they may be working on deadlines for grants and other important stuff." I responded by saying "*exactly*" and that's why I want students to visit their offices without an appointment because they are busy and under pressure. The lady went silent and had a puzzled look on her face. She was wondering why I would suggest dropping in on professors who are busy without an appointment. My point in visiting without an appointment is simply this—you need to see how your potential, future advisor will respond to you when he/she is extremely busy. I've knocked on professors' office doors before without an appointment and received at least two

If you do the smart things now, you will complete the Ph.D. degree

types of responses. One response was a very polite explanation of being too busy to see me and an appointment was scheduled for a later date. Another response was very rude and negative. The two types of responses gave me an indication of the persons' way of doing business and their character, at least when under pressure, the latter of which is certainly not a person I would want to have as my research advisor, guider, and mentor. I hope you get the point. As a college professor myself, I am always working on important paperwork and deadlines; however, when a student visits me, I believe that the student is more important than my paperwork. It's part of my character to put people first. Consider this: There are going to be times in which you MUST see your advisor IMMEDIATELY, and the situation doesn't permit you to delay; it needs to be NOW. Following through and doing this will give you an indication of how important you are to the potential future advisor. You are important, and you don't want to be at the bottom of the list in priorities.

At a recent conference I attended, I heard a speaker say, "We are to use things, and we are to love people." The point that the speaker was trying to get across was one of priority and the importance of people and how we should respond to people.

#6 Talk to past and present advisees

Talking to those who have personal experience of an advisor is worth its weight in gold. No one can give you better information than those who have been down, or are going down the road with an advisor. Junior and senior Ph.D. students are very knowledgeable in regards to who are "the good," "the bad" and "the ugly." Meet them and talk to them. Here are some suggested, unstructured interview questions to ask those students about their current advisor:

1. (assuming you know who their advisors are, ask).... I know that Professor X is your advisor, how long has she been your advisor?

2. I'm looking for an advisor myself. (Now be quiet and stay silent here and listen to how the student responds.

3. In your experience, is Professor X a good advisor?

4. What things do you like about Professor X?

5. What things do you not like about Professor X?

6. How often do the two of you meet?

7. Are you a part of her research team?

8. Would you recommend Professor X as a good advisor? Why or why not?

Go ahead and develop more questions that are specific to your program. Keep a record of the students' responses to your interview questions. Remember: If you don't write it down, you will not remember it.

Now at this point you should have narrowed down your choices to at least three to four potential advisors. It is now time for the BIG TEST. Contact each candidate, schedule a meeting and indicate to them that you want to discuss your interests and to get some advice. Your purpose of meeting with them is to interview them for the possibility of serving as your advisor. You can communicate this to them when you meet. It's important to be very respectful when you meet each of them. Initially, use the title Doctor when you address the professor. Then you may ask the potential advisors what they prefer that you call them; usually it will be Dr., Professor, Mr. or Ms., and sometimes they will indicate that you call them by their first name. I've learned that many new Ph.D. students feel uncomfortable addressing their professors by first name; however, if the individual requests it, then you do it regardless of how you feel. Several years ago, I had a professor who had recently completed her dissertation, graduated and was hired by the university as an assistant professor. A fellow student of mine met with her and called her by her first name. The

142

newly hired and freshly minted diploma professor was insulted to say the least. She responded to the student by saying, "My name is Dr. So and So. That student learned his lesson the hard way. So never make assumptions when addressing professors. Here are some good interview questions to ask and things to talk about when you meet each of the potential advisors. Begin the meeting by discussing the purpose of your meeting with them. Your purpose of meeting with them is to discuss your interest, their interest, and the <u>possibility of them serving as your</u> advisor if you both agree that it could be a profitable relationship.

Questions or rather Discussions Topics for Potential Advisors

1. Share your area of interest in research or your lack of having an area of interest.

2. Share with the professor what your current needs are (i.e., some directions, mentoring, completion of Program of Study forms, etc.)

3. Ask the potential advisors about their work or research agenda.

4. Assuming you attended their research group meetings, share some interest that you have related to what they are doing and/or your interest about some area of their published research work that you previously read.

5. Inquire about their current advisee load (Don't ask about paid assistantships. Expect them to mention it first; if they don't, then you do).

6. If the interview has been positive in terms of your assessment, then you need to ask towards the end of the interview the following question… "How interested would you be in serving as my research advisor?" Even if the person responds positively, you are not required to make an agreement at that point, and you shouldn't because you have others to interview before deciding. So don't allow your good feelings or pressure to make the decision. This decision needs to be a logical one.

End the interview by thanking the professor for his or her time. It's also good to let the professor know that you are looking for an advisor and that you will be meeting others in the department.

At this point, you have pin-pointed several potential advisors and identified their role in the department, you have attended their research group meetings, you have reviewed some of their published work, you have given them a copy of your work and you have gotten feedback, you have dropped by their offices unscheduled or without an appointment, you have communicated with some of their advisees, and you have interviewed or had personal meetings with each of the potential advisors. From the meetings with them, you have learned their research interests, their available resources, as well as determined if it would be a good working relationship. Now it's time to continue the elimination process. From the information that you have gathered, this should be quite easy.

List the names of the top two individuals, with your top preference first:

1. _____

2. _____

Meet again with these two professors to discuss with each about joining their team. If you get positive responses from both, then pray, and choose one.

Getting the most out of the relationship with your advisor

Now that you have an advisor, you want the relationship to benefit you. Too many graduate students do not seek the things that they need from the relationship. They only meet the requirement by choosing an advisor. What good does it do to have an advisor and not take advantage of his or her experience? Every program is different. If this person is your research advisor, you will be working closely with him or her, especially if you get a position of research assistant. My plan on how to get the most from the relationship includes doing the following:

- ✓ Meet regularly, once weekly or once every two weeks
- ✓ Prepare for your meetings

1) List topics to discuss.
2) Identify what you want to get out of the meeting.
3) Give summary of what you have done since the last meeting.
4) Discuss any important deadlines.
5) Set date and time for next meeting.

✓ E-mail your advisor a summary of every meeting. In the e-mail note the following:

1) Identify what you understood from the meeting.
2) Identify what your assignments are.
3) Date and time agreed upon for next meeting.

Important is that you always be proactive in the advising relationship. Take charge and get things done. Come up with your own ideas and share them. Start developing your interests and learn all you can about them.

Remember you do not have to always agree with everything that your advisor says. When you disagree, state your concerns clearly. If you feel like something is going well, communicate it. Take the initiative in the relationship. You are a doctoral student, and to be successful you must be a person who is responsible and willing to take action on important matters. You do not need your advisor's advice on everything.

Hot Points

Identify important information that you need to refer back to.

_____

_____

_____

_____

_____

_____

_____

_____

If you do the smart things now, you will complete the Ph.D. degree

Chapter 8

Your Second Year in Ph.D. Program

"You see, in life, lots of people know what to do, but few
people actually do what they know. Knowing is not enough!
You must take action."
Anthony Robbins

"It is common sense to take a method and try it. If it fails,
admit it frankly and try another. But above all, try something."
Franklin D. Roosevelt

The second year in your Ph.D. program is an exciting year.
You have accomplished much in your first full year: choosing an
advisor, taking courses, and learning to do research. The
foundation is now laid and you are building upon it. By now, you
should have a very good understanding of what's going on and
what you should be doing. Let's make sure that you have done
those important things in your first year. Place a check by the
items below indicating what you have completed.

Read Departmental Handbook   ( )

Developed an Annual Calendar   ( )

Applied for Financial Assistance   ( )

If you do the smart things now, you will complete the Ph.D. degree

Developed a Program of Study for the entire program	( )
Equivalent Master level hours have been transferred into Ph.D. Program	( )
Worked as a Research Assistant	( )
Applied for a Graduate Teaching Assistant Position	( )
Identified and am reading professional journals in your area	( )
Selected your advisor	( )

If there are any items above that are not checked off as completed, then you need to take care of those items now. Procrastination is mother of not winning.

Your second year in the Ph.D. program consists of what I call "functioning as a graduate student." You are busy, you have completed your first year, and now you are just doing the things you need to be doing. I've identified eight specific things you need to do now that you are in your second year. I would say that these eight functions operate across disciplines for all Ph.D.

students. Below is a list of the eight functions with detailed explanations to follow.

- Balance schedule and assistantship
- Meet Regularly with your advisor
- Get involved in research
- Function within your capacity
- Network
- Attend conferences
- Maintain high ethical standards

Balance Schedule and Assistantship

In your first year, if you applied for an assistantship to teach or to do research with a professor, then you are now matriculating in your own classes and teaching undergraduate students or doing research. Unless you are superman or superwoman, you don't want to overburden yourself with studying for your own classes and at the same time <u>teaching undergraduates</u> and working as a <u>research assistant</u>. That's tooooo heavy of a load for most.

It's important that you don't allow yourself to get caught in the trap of trying to take on too many classes in a given semester or term. If you are doing an assistantship, I suggest enrolling in no more than three courses—maybe even two classes if your assistantship requires more than twenty hours of your time per

152

week. It just depends on how much you can handle. The first semester in my assistantship, I chose to enroll in two classes because those two classes required a great of my time doing research and writing. A balanced schedule will consider the volume of your course work, academic readings, time spent in your assistantship, and all non-academic related activities.

If you are about to work as a graduate teaching assistant, I have some very valuable information to share with you. I remember my first teaching assignment. It was not a pleasant thought. My brain and body came up with some amazing thoughts and actions. Those thoughts were of fear, nervousness, and inadequacy; and my body was shaken with fear. I knew the students would see me as frightful and unknowledgeable. When given the assignment to teach, I went out and bought books on how to teach students at the college level. I even attended a workshop on how to teach because I was determined not to make a fool of myself in front of a class. Psychologists have said that public speaking is the number one fear among all people. I definitely fit the description of a person who feared public speaking. The valuable information that I have for you to help you succeed as a teacher is what I used to give myself confidence in front of the class. This information gives guidance on what you need to avoid while in the classroom. I found this information in the Journal of Teaching Psychology, authored by William Buskist. The article indicated that Buskist observed new graduate teaching assistants

teach for over a decade. He noticed the students making simple
mistakes that can be avoided. Use the list below as information to
make yourself a better teacher and to avoid common errors. I'm
going to tell the whole truth here; the absolute truth is that I have
seen experienced teachers and even full-tenured professors make
these mistakes. Take these ten common mistakes that teaching
assistants make and avoid them.

Ten Common Teaching Mistakes TA's (and Veterans) Make

1. Starting class cold – "Today we are going to talk about x and
here's the first of five definitions for it." No time for small talk or
side comments—hit that content and hit it hard. Buskist suggests
developing a warm-up. He offers these questions to assist the
effort. "Are students already familiar with this concept? Is there
an everyday example I could use to pique students' interest in the
concept? How might the concept relate to recent events in
students' lives?"

2. Reviewing graded materials at the beginning of class –
Deliver the bad news first, get it out of the way, and move on into
the comfort of important content. It works for the teacher but
leaves students mulling over the feedback and not focused on the
material. Save the graded stuff for last and welcome students who
have points to argue to join you for private conversation after class.

3. Projecting a weak presence – Most beginning teachers feel uncomfortable and look it. Images of timidity, awkwardness, and indecisiveness will be taken as signs of weakness that students have been known to take advantage of. Consider having your teaching taped and getting some expert opinions when you view the tape.

4.Weakly integrating major points – Beginning teachers generally have major points, but they don't have effective links and connections between them. Buskist has another set of questions that will help you develop transitions and a more coherent whole. "How can I link these topics together? Is there an example or demonstration I can use to link these topics? What questions might I pose to help students see such linkages?"

5. Relying too heavily on notes – New teachers write detailed notes. Recent or current students themselves, they are used to writing long complicated sentences about content meant to be read not heard. When they read those notes to students, they can quickly bore even a motivated crowd. Solution: Make an outline of the material. Put it on the board or overhead and lecture from that. It has the added advantage of helping students organize their notes.

6. Not talking to the class – New teachers have a tendency to talk to the board or read from the overhead. In this culture (and most others), we face people and speak to them directly.

7. Giving ambiguous demonstrations – Demonstrations are an excellent, active learning technique with great potential for getting students' attention and making important points in the process. Those benefits accrue only if the point of the demonstration is clear.

8. Posing vague questions – Often the "vague" question is really just a very open one designed to give students lots of latitude when they respond. Unfortunately, they don't know that. They believe that all questions have right answers and since they don't know the answer to this one, they must not understand the question. Buskist includes an example of a vague question: "What do we know about attribution?" Compare that question with these more effective ones: "What are the key elements of attributions?" or "In attribution, what is the relationship among consensus, consistency, and distinctiveness?"

9. Not reinforcing student participation – Ignore student comments, or take them for granted, and you won't have them for long. This doesn't mean making much out of an inferior or incorrect answer, but is does mean acknowledging student effort and giving praise when it is merited.

10. Not repeating students' question or comments – Especially a problem in large classes, shy students aren't sure they want to be participating in this big class anyway. They speak quietly so that even the instructor can barely make out the answer. Repeat the answer, or ask the student or someone else to say it again so that everyone can hear. Even your most eloquent answer makes little sense if students don't start out knowing the question.

Avoiding these simple teaching mistakes is worth its weight in gold. You can become a very good teacher through practice. Consider practice teaching in front of a mirror or use a made-up audience consisting of your friends and family members. Remember, practice does not make perfect, but it does make improvements.

Meet Regularly with Advisor

Regular meetings with your advisor are something that I
strongly advise. Just because you are in your second year and you
now know more, don't make the mistake of thinking you've got it
all together and meeting your advisor on a regular basis is not
necessary. It is necessary. During your first year you were
learning the ropes and setting your agenda with your advisor's
guidance, but now it's time to advance your research and start
thinking dissertation. Ooops, did I mention dissertation? We'll get
to that later. Set goals with your advisor on what you should be
accomplishing in this second year. A relevant agenda for
discussions with your advisor includes talking about

- Your teaching and teaching techniques
- Research hours and related tasks
- Progression in your course work
- Doing research and publications
- Dissertation interests and topics

Get Involved in Research

Generally speaking, the Ph.D. degree is a research degree, and
most who pursue it tend to lean towards careers entering into the
professoriate, academic positions, or some other area of research.
Most programs or even your program will place a heavy emphasis
on research. But since the Ph.D. typically requires completing a

dissertation, you need to delve more deeply into learning how to do research around your second year. Your first year laid the foundation in taking courses and learning the ropes and developing your specific area of interest. Becoming more involved in research will be your journey from here till the end of your program and even into your career.

Allow me to share something with you that I typically share in my talks and lectures. The Ph.D. degree is the highest degree that one can earn. Those with Ph.D.'s are the real doctors and those with medical degrees (M.D.) and jurist doctorates (J.D.) are not really doctors at all. Medical doctors are like automobile mechanics. An auto mechanic will lift the hood of a car, replace parts, and make the car run better. An attorney will look at a case and review what has been done in the past on similar cases and then argue his case before a judge and jury. In those fields of work, all one has to learn to do is to fix something or argue something. The real intellectuals and scholars are Ph.D.s. We are the ones who impact our society and future through understanding human behaviors, histories, mankind, ideals and the like.

I have been criticized for making such claims about who the real doctors are.

In doing research you are on the path to making a tremendous difference in the world. If you are on target, you have learned quite a bit in your first year. During your first year you spent time taking courses from different professors in your department as well as outside of your department. Also, you learned about several professors' research agenda while you were investigating to match yourself with an advisor. Now it's time to really connect with someone to go even further with research. By your second year, you should have knowledge of the research agenda of every professor in your department research agenda. If you don't know all of their agendas, you can do several things to find out. For example, you can inquire directly of them, or you can go to their web-site which may list their work, or you can seek their published work.

List the names of all of your department's professor and their research agenda.

Professor's Names   Research Agendas

_____

_____

_____

_____

_____   _____

_____   _____

_____   _____

_____   _____

_____   _____

Now list the names and research agendas of those professors who
are not in your department, but about whose research work you
have an interest. Remember, I found a research advisor outside of
my department because his work was more in line with what I
wanted to do.

Outside Professors' Names   Research Agendas

_____   _____

_____   _____

_____   _____

_____   _____

Many Ph.D. students will do research with their advisor since a close relationship has developed in the first year. However, as you review the list of agendas above, you may have more interest in someone other than your advisor. During my graduate school years I had very little interest in the work that professors were doing in my major department and specific college as a whole. One professor's research agenda focused on "Internal Knowledge," another focused on a Russian scientist named Lev Vygotsky, and others had focuses that just didn't move, motivate, or interest me. Therefore, I chose to do work with someone from another department and school on the university campus. Dr. Steve Nagy was his name. I met Dr. Nagy by way of taking a course from his wife, Dr. Christine Nagy. During class she made mention of a grant that her husband was working on that involved assisting youth through developing training and mentoring programs. She told me that he was looking for someone to work on the project with him. I immediately contacted him by phone and we met and talked about his research and my interests. Needless to say, I found my calling. My final two years in the Ph.D. program focused on doing research with Dr. Nagy and developing training programs. Now, today that is exactly what I'm doing. So, as you can see, it's important that you search your university and learn what others are doing and seek to build a relationship with a professor whose work interests you.

How to find my Area

Research is an interesting animal. The truth is most of what's going on in research is not new stuff, but rather, a way of expanding what we already know. That will always be a good thing to do. So, you never need to approach research as if you must come up with some unknown or revolutionary idea or some unheard of finding. Unless you can find a cure for cancer, you will probably add to or come from a different perspective in some area of research that's already being done. Now, look back over the previous exercise in which you listed professors' names and research agendas that work in and outside of your department. List at least three of those professors and their research agendas that strike you as possible individuals to work with.

Professor's Names	**Research Agendas**
1. _____	_____
2. _____	_____
3. _____	_____

Next, write out why you are interested in their work. This is important because it helps you to think about why or for what reason you want to go in a particular direction.

_____

_____

_____

_____

_____

_____

_____

_____

_____

_____

If you do the smart things now, you will complete the Ph.D. degree

_____

_____

Unless you already have a good grasp of what those three
individuals are doing, I suggest that you learn more about their
research before approaching any one of them to inquire about
joining their team or asking them to direct your research. By the
way, my dissertation was on the project that I worked on with Dr.
Steve Nagy. He was wonderful to work with.

Function within your capacity

All too often I've seen Ph.D. students get caught in the trap
of taking on more than they can handle. I learned that doctoral
students seem to be called on to do many extra academic duties. It
just goes with the territory. You may be asked to teach several
courses, to work on research projects with more than one
professor, to take the leadership role of some project, or to join
several committees or clubs, and other assignments. Be careful in
what you select to do. It's easy to spread yourself too thin among
all of those who may request your help. Doing too much will
cause burnout and frustration. Typically, a lot of these different
opportunities will be coming your way during your second year in
the program, so be mindful and don't over do it.

Network

Networking for doctoral students will be one of your most powerful tools. In your second year you need to expand your horizons. Start building relationships with others. Learn what others are doing in your department and outside of your department. The benefits of networking with professors, students, administrators and individuals outside of the university will pay off. I remember during the second year of my program at the University of Alabama, I needed some valuable information, and through a contact that I had, I was connected to a professor at the University of Mississippi. He and I communicated, and I got exactly what I needed. Getting to know others will expand your horizon. I know of many Ph.D. students who began to network inside and outside of their university and were able to land faculty positions throughout the country. Another great way to network is to attend conferences.

Start Writing your Dissertation

See chapter ten.

Attend Conferences and Seminars

There will be many opportunities to attend conferences to learn, to meet people, and to present your work. A major part of being a doctoral student is attending these meetings that are related to your area or major. My major in graduate school was educational psychology, and there are several psychology-related organizations. These entities have their annual conferences throughout the country. The American Psychological Association (APA) has its meetings every year at different and exciting places throughout the country. It's important to attend some of these conferences. Initially, your advisor will be the person to gather information on which conference and seminar to attend. Then later, as you learn more you will be able to decide which conference is best for you. Attending these meetings, you will learn what others are doing in your field, and you will attend workshops geared towards learning and improving your abilities as a researcher. Talk to your advisor about joining him or her at some of these events.

Are you familiar with what organizations or associations are out there for your major or research area? If you answered yes, then list them below; if you don't know, then you need to ask your advisor.

Speak with your advisor and department professors to learn the names of organizations that are related to your major. List those organizations here:

_____

_____

_____

_____

_____

I hope that you have at least five. Now, search their Websites to learn more about the organization. Then you want to find out the dates of their upcoming conferences and list the information and locations on your calendar. If you do some good networking, you may find the monies to help cover your travel expense and fees to attend these meetings.

Maintain High Ethical Standards

High ethical standards include being a person of integrity and honesty, and having a good reputation. You may ask me what I'm talking about here. Well, as you delve more deeply into research, teaching classes, taking courses, writing papers, attending conferences and doing all the other things that Ph.D. students are required to do, you will begin to see and/or hear about unscrupulous behaviors that a few Ph.D. students do to gain an extra advantage. There is a bunch of politicking in graduate school. For instance, I know of students who have said negative and untrue things about others to authority figures to make themselves look good. That's WRONG! But it is a reality. Some will step on others to get ahead. Because graduate school is so very competitive, some students will steal others' work or not give credit. That's called plagiarism. It is probably the biggest sin that Ph.D. students commit. You should never write a paper of any kind using the findings of others as if it were your own. Words for the wise— if you get caught cheating, you may be expelled, kicked out, given your pink slip, sent on your way. No matter what, don't be tempted to plagiarize. A good code of ethics is always to be honest. If you are not 100% certain on what qualifies as plagiarism, then talk with your advisor or better yet, show the advisor your paper and identify to him in the paper any borderline items that may be labeled stealing.

Recently, I had an incident to occur in my Human Growth and Development course. Students enrolled in this class are required to turn in a portfolio at semester's end. This portfolio is to consist of research, writings, interviews, and carrying out simple experiments. I caught plagiarism in one of my student's assignments. Nothing upsets me more than cheating and stealing. After speaking to the student so that I could hear her side, she "Swore before God" that she didn't know that copying someone else's work and changing a few words in it was plagiarism. My options were to expel her from the college or give her an "F" in course. I'm soft hearted, so I chose the latter. I believe that there are rewards for those who work hard and operate under integrity and honesty. I learned a great deal about honesty and integrity from my wife Angel. She epitomizes honesty and integrity. I remember once she had to leave her job at a local hospital to take care of a small business matter for which she would be away for only about ten to fifteen minutes. She signed off the clock when she left and signed back on when she returned. I asked her why she would clock out for a ten-to-fifteen-minute errand. She said, "Because it is the right thing to do, and I would never even want to give the appearance of being dishonest even if I could easily get away it." I thought WOW, this woman is amazing. But I learned from her that little things are important and that it just pays to be in the right. That same year, she received an award from the hospital as "The Best Team Member." So keep in mind always to do the right thing.

As you continue to progress in the program at this point, you need to continue to think about your dissertation. Your work and courses you are taking should be closely in line with your dissertation. So throughout your program select courses that build around your research interests and your dissertation.

Hot Points

Identify important information that you need to refer back to.

_____

_____

_____

_____

_____

_____

_____

_____

If you do the smart things now, you will complete the Ph.D. degree

Chapter 9

Ten Common Mistakes Made by Ph.D. Students

"Keys to success.....Research your idea, Plan for success,
Expect success, and just plain do it! It amazes me how
many people skip the last step! Practice being a "doer"
and success will follow you every step of the way."
Josh S. Hinds

"True success is not what you have or what you can
do, but true success is what did you do with what you
have, in other words, how many people have you helped
to win in life?"
Samuel Jones

Now that you are in a Ph.D. program, it's time to get serious. You are going to invest your time, energy, and money so you might as well give 100% of yourself to the effort. This chapter will outline the ten common mistakes that Ph.D. students make and offer sure problem fixer so that you won't travel these paths. Experience is not the best teacher, so if you can learn from others' mistakes and prevent them from happening to you, that's the BEST teacher.

Common Mistakes:

1) Working, playing, or socializing too much and studying too little. Upon your acceptance into graduate school, you have made a commitment. It's important that you balance your life and do your work. Schoolwork must be first; playing and socializing should come as a reward for doing an excellent job when you succeed at the small steps along the way.

2) Not using good time management skills – you must be organized and structured with your assignments and meeting deadlines if you are serious about earning a doctorate degree.

3) Not attending departmental and program's students meetings – these meetings are for your benefit and to keep you up to date. Go to these meetings to learn the important things about what's going on.

4) Not meeting with advisor to confirm that you are taking the right courses and in the right sequence—meet with your advisor regularly to examine where you are and what you should be doing

5) Taking on too much responsibilities—be careful, because you may be asked to join more than a few committees and to take on other leadership roles. Too much of this can hinder your progress.

6) Not seeking help when needed – many graduate students do not seek help because they do not want to appear to be weak in a highly competitive environment. VERY UNWISE! SEEK HELP WHENEVER NEEDED.

If you do the smart things now, you will complete the Ph.D. degree

7) Not balancing schoolwork and personal life – it's important that you have balance in your life. Schoolwork is important, but it will suffer if you do not allow time for other activities. Yes, this includes having some fun.

8) Waiting until the last minute to locate important journal articles, books, other readings - the quality of your work will suffer if you procrastinate and cram to turn in assignments.

9) Not politically astute – the graduate students who get needed resources, money, and opportunities know how to: a) locate and meet the right people, b) communicate, and c) do their homework.

10) Don't be an "Air Head" – by now you should know and be able to communicate intelligently with any one who asks about your personal and professional goals.

My Ph.D. is in educational psychology. My master's degree is in counseling. For many years I have had an interest in personalities and what makes people tick. My specific interest is in personality disorders. A personality disorder can be defined as a collection of traits (consistent ways of thinking and behaving) that deviate or is different from the social norm (what's acceptable). No, this is not "a writing" on abnormal psychology, but I'm convinced that everybody to some degree is abnormal.

When your friends and associates learn that you are working on your Ph.D. or applying for a Ph.D. program, they will immediately think differently of you. Notice their reactions. Immediately, they will lavish upon you admiration, praise, and encouragement. They will be very supportive. They will say, "that's great," "I'm happy for you," and "you can do it." However, and on the inside they will think:

Why is (he, she) going to go for a Ph.D.?

Isn't (he, she) happy already?

I would never spend that much time and money going for a Ph.D.

(He, She) will never make it.

Those with Ph.D. degrees are not normal.

Since none of us are normal, especially doctoral students, I'll share my disorder with you. Yes, that's right I have a disorder. I have obsessive compulsive disorder or OCD, an anxiety disorder. During my Ph.D. years (all 6 ½ of them), I suffered with a moderate case of OCD brought on by doing Ph.D. work. In short, obsessions are thoughts and images that intrude and remain constant in your mind, sometimes causing stress, worry, or great concern. Compulsions are things that you do repetitively and consistently, hoping to lower the anxiety associated with the thing you are overly concerned with.

I was obsessed for 6 ½ years with not failing and not succeeding in graduate school. The possibility of failing and not doing my best triggered symptoms of anxiety in me. Not doing well was not an option for me. I thought on these things all of the time. My compulsions or behaviors made me not over extend my social life. My compulsions made me spend hours, and hours, and hours in the university library doing my work, staying up to 3:00 o'clock on many mornings, making sure that that research paper was the best it could it be.

I was so obsessed with doing well to the point that I would literally sneak in some reading of research articles at those long, boring traffic lights; you know the ones that take forever to change from red to green. Early in my marriage, when taking my wife out to dinner, I would catch up on some much needed reading while we were waiting to be seated. I quickly learned that that was something that she was not going to tolerate. My wife would insist, sometimes with attitude, that I put that textbook or article away and enjoy an evening with her. I had to learn not to be so obsessed with succeeding. Nevertheless, it is absolutely necessary that you develop some symptoms associated with OCD in order to be successful so that you won't make the ten common mistakes that graduate students often make.

Types of Students

Graduate school is a different animal than undergraduate. For many undergraduate students it is a time of coming into adulthood and exploration. Some of these students think that college life is a party. And, many will party and party and party, then later regret how much time was wasted not giving their absolute best. But that's okay, because grad school is only for the serious and mature student and for those who grew into maturity during their first four years of college. In grad school you are more focused, you know what you want to do, and you are more committed. I heard this funny story about commitment. A man and his wife were having breakfast at a Denny's restaurant. When the waiter came, the man ordered some bacon and eggs and his wife ordered cereal. When the server brought out their food, the man asked his wife to look at the bacon and eggs, on his plate. She looked. He told her that the chicken made a contribution, but the pig was totally committed. The pig had to give up his life to make that meal possible. Many undergraduate students do not see commitment as a key trait; they see themselves and attending school as making a contribution to the university process. But, on the other hand, grad students do not have a choice; they must be committed. In a sense, undergraduate students are chickens, and Ph.D. students are pigs. So join the crowd, Oink Oink.

Avoiding the Temptations

Let's look back on eight of the common mistakes mentioned (skipping 5 and 7):

1. playing and socializing too much
2. poor time management skills
3. not attending meetings
4. not meeting with advisor
6. not seeking help when needed
8. waiting until the last minute to do work
9. not being politically astute
10. not being able to communicate goals

I have observed all of the above in some graduate students. I too have made some of these mistakes. Any one of them can become a habit that costs too much. It's easy to be tempted to do things that you shouldn't do and to be tempted to not do things that you should do. Mistakes that I made early in my graduate school years were #3 (not attending meetings) and #6 (not seeking help when needed). By not attending departmental meetings I missed out on learning important information about the happenings within the department and I missed out on research opportunities, important campus events, and monies that were available. I thought going to those meetings was just a waste of my time and that my time would be better spent doing some other important stuff. Often times and weeks later I would learn from others (after the meeting) of benefits that I could have gotten had I been there. I missed out on some valuable publications *(you know what I mean, not signing on to work with someone on a publishable piece of work)* because I chose not to avail myself for meetings.

Secondly, I made the mistake of not seeking help when needed. We all need help. But I thought that because I was a doctoral student, I should already be perfect; and I should already know the answers to everything. That was S-T-U-P-I-D on my part. In my first two years I made many mistakes by not asking for and seeking help. You must not let pride get in your way.

Around my third year in the program, after learning how stupid I was, I became wiser. I started attending all meetings. In fact, the next year I was selected and served as the president of our student government association of our department; now I was running and organizing the meetings. I began to ask any and everybody questions who I thought would know the answers. I became a regular in visiting professors with my questions and ideas.

Identify four mistakes that you made in undergraduate school and list them

---

_____

_____

_____

Mistakes are costly. For each mistake that you wrote down, write below what you lost or what it cost you.

_____

_____

_____

_____

Finally, if you could do it all over again, what would you do differently.

_____

_____

It's okay that you made some mistakes in your past; the important thing is whether you learned from them and what you will do differently now. Posing this assignment to you takes me back to when I was an undergraduate, majoring in psychology. I did not work as diligently as I could have in my Psychology of Physiology course. I hated that course. I hated having to dissect sheep brains. I hated learning the parts of the brain and their function. I hated the professor, and I hated going to class. Because of my foolishness I made a fat and well deserved "D" in that course—no one's fault but mine.

Abnormal Personality

Now, back to my obsessive compulsive personality disorder. To be obsessed is not crazy. It simply is to have persistent thoughts, ideas, impulses, or images at the forefront of one's consciousness, whereas compulsions are repeated behaviors that the individuals feel they must perform to reduce those persistent thoughts, ideas, impulses, and images. I believe that a mild case of OCD is a healthy personality for Ph.D. students. You do not have the luxury of procrastinating and not being focused. You MUST get things done. Having a mild case of OCD

If you do the smart things now, you will complete the Ph.D. degree

regarding being excellent towards my course work—research papers, exams, teaching, doing research kept me on target. I was always thinking about what needed to be done and when. Also, I always thought about giving my best effort in whatever I did. I kept a full calendar of what was coming so that I could complete assignments/tasks before they were due.

Thoughts and images would often intrude into my mind about failing, and they did not feel good. I was concerned about keeping an excellent grade point average and performing at the same level as others in the program whom I thought and just assumed were much smarter than I. Sometime it's good to be bothered with negative thoughts to push past being lethargic and being inactive. It's relatively easy to develop this type of personality or at least some of the symptoms. I hope you can see that you need to be concerned about your work and doing well.

I have two simple techniques that work. I did both of these exercises while in my program, and they helped create within me the characteristics associated with OCD and ultimately led to my success. For these two techniques to work, three factors must be present. Those three factors are the following:

- you must know what it is that you want to do with your life
- you must be passionate about having it, and
- you must feel dread and pain not to have it.

182

Technique #1: Write down the six most important things that you will lose if you don't succeed in your Ph.D. program:

1. _____

2. _____

3. _____

4. _____

5. _____

6. _____

After you have identified the six most important things that you would lose if you don't succeed, take some time now to imagine your life without completing the degree. Picture what you are doing and be very specific (IMPORTANT: *I didn't say, picture what you will be doing; I said picture what you are doing **in the present tense***), imagine the money you are making doing it, and think about what you have and don't have because of your not succeeding. Now go ahead and allow yourself to experience the pain of this loss. When I did this same exercise during my graduate school years, I pictured myself working in an eight to five job at an office desk and **HATING** every moment of it. If you met the three criteria of knowing what you want to do with your life, feeling passion about it, and experiencing pain and dread if you don't achieve it, then, when you picture yourself without it, you should feel pain, regret, and a huge disappointment.

Write down how this exercise affected you:

_____

_____

_____

_____

The second part of this exercise is more positive and is the fun side.

Technique #2: Write down what you will gain by completing your doctorate degree:

1. _____

2. _____

3. _____

4. _____

5. _____

6. _____

Now that you have listed six things that you will gain by completing your degree, imagine yourself in the future with the degree, and answer the following questions:

How do you feel? _____

What are you doing? _____

How much money are you making? _____

Who else is benefiting from your success? _____

The reward of achievement is a great motivator. I did this exact same exercise, and it made me feel incredible. I pictured myself in the professoriate. I saw me impacting every student in my classes.

If you do the smart things now, you will complete the Ph.D. degree

I saw me specializing in a particular area and doing workshops around the nation. I saw me writing books and presenting workshops to help people. Guess what? All of those things are now true. I absolutely love helping people and making a difference in their lives. My biggest weakness is an extremely strong desire to help people. I label that a weakness because I tend to have a 'persistent-and- never-give up attitude and actions' toward people who need help but don't want help. Sometimes I can be too overbearing with my positive attitude and motivations and easily begin to annoy people who want me just to leave them alone and allow them to fail or suffer. For example, there was a young girl I knew who completed her bachelor's degree in criminal justice with a desire to go on to law school and become a successful attorney. However, she never took the initiative to apply to law school and was not succeeding in her career as a paralegal. Again and again and again, I would communicate with her about practicing and studying the LSAT (Law School Admission Test) and applying to law school. She promised she would but took no actions. Every time I tried to motivate her to take actions, she either said "I will" or gave an excuse as to why she couldn't go. I believe excuses are the main reason that people will not live up to their full potential. They say things like "I don't have enough money" or "I'm too old" or "no one in family has ever achieve anything" or "I don't have the time." These excuses remind me of a story about a man who had many talents (or money) and he went out and chose three men and gave each of them some of his talents. One man was given five talents another three and another one. The man who received five talents went out an invested them and doubled his return to the tone of ten. The man who received three talents also went out and invested and doubled his talents to the tone of six. However, the man who received only one talent did nothing. He buried his talent in the ground for safe keeping. When the owner returned to see how well the men used the talents given them, he was satisfied with the two men who invested their talents and very dissatisfied with the man who did not use his talent. Too many people are like that third man; they are not using what they already have and will live the rest of theirs lives not reaching their maximum potential. I didn't stop with this young lady because I had no doubt that she had the qualities to be a successful lawyer. I encouraged this young lady about getting her law degree and even went so far as to provide literature about law school. She said that she would make the calls, but didn't. I continued to be relentless in my effort to get this person to take action, but none was ever taken.

I live by this motto:

"I, Samuel Jones, would rather attempt something great and fail than not to attempt at all." Don't you agree with that? Put your name in the parentheses and say this. *I*

(your name) would rather attempt something great and fail than not to attempt at all.

Make that your confession; make that your lifestyle.

Success or Failure

In my working with people and through my own experiences, I have learned something that amazes me. It amazes me because I am a person who finds it easy to take risks, to burn the bridges behind me, to go for what I want in life. Sometimes you have to go for what you want in life even at the expense of people's not understanding or not believing in you. When I decided to pursue a Ph.D. from the University of Alabama, I was told by a man whom I loved and admired that I should not go to that university. He explained to me that blacks do not do well at that university, and he reminded me about the incidence that occurred years ago when former Governor George Wallace stood in the doorway of Rose Hall not allowing blacks to attend the university. Well his words did not deter my determination. I went and succeeded in spite of that. In my years I've learned that most people have a greater fear of failure than success. In other words, most people will do more to not lose something that they already have, than doing more to gain something that they don't have, because they fear failure. For example, "I'm gonna keep my money in my pocket and not invest to earn more because I might

If you do the smart things now, you will complete the Ph.D. degree

lose it." Let me share an early experience about my life with you. I'm almost embarrassed to put this in print, but when I look back and think about it, it inspires me to remember how much I wanted to succeed in life. Let me add this: Successful people that you meet in life are pretty much just like anyone else. The difference is that they have experienced lots of failures, but didn't give up and kept on trying something new. You must be willing to fail again and again and again in order to experience true success. Read on about these two experiences and think about your own life and what have you attempted in your past.

Shortly after graduating from high school, I decided to move out west to California, land of big dreams and big opportunities. I was eager, hungry and just ready to take on the world. I was confident that California was waiting for my arrival. It was my plan to be the next discovered star. I expected the red carpet to be laid out for my arrival. So at the young age of nineteen and with my life savings of about $1200, I moved out there and found myself a one-room motel to live in. As the days went by, I found a couple of jobs breading shrimp in the early mornings at a Red Lobster restaurant and flipping hamburgers at Wendy's Old Fashion Hamburgers during the nights. I was content for a while, but I was looking and searching for my big break.

During this time in the early eighties Michael Jackson had just released his top selling album Thriller. It was the biggest selling recording ever. All the radio stations and everybody loved MJ. Growing up as a child I had always been a big Michael Jackson and Jackson Five fan from the early 70's. And when he became so huge in the 80's, and I happened to be in California, I felt it was my opportunity to take advantage of my purpose for moving to California, to be rich and famous. I began to practice hours upon hours upon hours, dancing and singing like Michael Jackson. I watched all the videos of him that I could get my hands on. I watched all his appearances on television, and I even went to see him in concert twice. I had mastered all of his dance moves including the famous "moonwalk." Well, shortly thereafter I had a friend to curl and style my hair, do makeup on my face, and I began to travel the state of California entering different competitions and shows performing as Michael Jackson. One of my performances was at the world famous Disneyland Hotel in Anaheim. I was doing great and earning money for my appearances. After performing, people would actually come up to me and call me Michael and even ask for my autograph. I was that good! One night while performing in a city call Torrance, outside of Los Angeles, a popular show coordinator saw me and was impressed. He asked me if I would be interested in taping a performance for the popular show at that time called Solid Gold. I was thrilled. I knew in my heart that this was it. I would be a star. I did a tape for the show, and it was aired on the weekend for a national television audience. In my humble opinion I was

OUTSTANDING. After the show I received calls from family and friends from around the country. I continued to perform as MJ in night club joints and for other events around town. Then something happened. MJ's popularity and the public's interest in others who imitated him began to shift downward. So there went my MJ career. But I did not give up. I was determined to find my niche.

Another person whom I admired was Arnold Swarznegger, truly the greatest bodybuilder who ever lived. Since the age of thirteen I was an Arnold Swarznegger fan. When I was a very young thirteen year old, I began bodybuilding and was heavily into reading all of the muscle magazines. During my high school years, I tried out for football and baseball. However, I just did not have the skills to perform on the level needed. But in the weight room I was good, and I fell absolutely in love with lifting weights and continued to lift weights throughout high school.

While living in my motel in a city called Buena Park, in California, and within a few days of living in California, I borrowed a friend's car, got directions and drove to the world famous Gold's gym located in Santa Monica near Venice Beach. With my enthusiasm flowing, I went inside the gym, talking to and interrupting anybody who would listen to me. I asked the staff behind the counters and the bodybuilders who were training where I could find Arnold Swarzennegger, and that I wanted to talk with him. I'm sure they thought that this country-accented teenager was crazy. But with my zeal, I knew that if Arnold would take me under his arms, I would be a huge superstar bodybuilder. Unfortunately, he wasn't around and I've never gotten the opportunity to meet him.

Well in 1991 and after my MJ career ended, Arnold Swarzennegger came out with his second Terminator movie. I went to see it on its first day out, standing in a line that stretched around the theater and waiting at least two hours for tickets. I just had to see it at any cost. The movie was a mega hit. In my mind but with no serious thoughts of taking any action, I secretly thought that I could be the next Arnold Swarzennegger. I was already working out four days per week, but now I began to work out with weights on a daily basis. Sometime around May in 1993, I was approached by a man named Rick who saw me training in the gym. Rick was the producer of one of the biggest bodybuilding competitions in California, the Orange County Muscle Classic. He approached me in the gym and asked me how long I had been working out with weights. I told him since the age of thirteen. Rick went on to say that I looked very good and he asked me to compete in his upcoming bodybuilding competition in August. My mind went wild. I was thrilled!!!! I knew that being the next Arnold was near. With only three months left to train and prepare for the August show, I worked out early in the mornings and returned to the gym in the evenings. I went on a strict diet to be in the best shape that I could possibly be. I was determined to not just put on a good show, but I was intent on winning and moving up to even bigger and possibly national competitions. Rick thought I had a good chance of winning my division. He would visit the gym to teach me how to pose and how to flex my muscles. I felt prepared and ready.

Well, the day of the competition finally arrived. When my name was called to appear on stage, I looked out at the audience with stage fright was all over my face. There were over fifteen hundred people in that Anaheim arena with television cameras and photographers everywhere. I began to wonder why I was there. I was filled with fear. There I stood dressed in nothing but tight bikini underwear with my body drenched in baby oil. I was scared to death. I walked on stage to do my ninety second routine. Nervousness and tension were all over me. I did my best to hide it from the cameras and audience. To this very day, I enjoy going back, pulling out that old video and watching that pitiful performance from my first show. Out of about twelve bodybuilders in my weight division, I placed fifth. I was happy to have placed fifth and was even more pumped up to train and compete again. Placing fifth to me was very good because it was only my first show. I was on an incredible high.

I continued to compete in other shows with my highest placing being third. One of my competitions was broadcasted on television. Shortly thereafter, I noticed things happening in the gym and in the sport around me, and I became discouraged and retired from bodybuilding. My discouragement was not necessarily related to my low placing in shows, but rather, I noticed that many of the bodybuilders in my weight class were using steroids and other drugs to gain an advantage. I felt it was wrong for users to compete against non-users like me because it gave them an unfair advantage. So I left the sport.

What was my purpose in sharing my early experiences as a performer and as a bodybuilder? I have a twofold purpose. First, do you remember the young girl who wanted to go to law school but would not take the initiative, and the friend who advised me not to go to the University of Alabama because I would fail? I believe that it is vital that you **pursue your dreams** no matter what. It doesn't matter if there is a greater possibility for failure. It doesn't matter if the odds are against you. As I think back, it's not easy breaking into show business or being the next great bodybuilder. But pursuing those things has created within me a mental recording in my unconscious that speaks to my conscious and tells me that if I'm willing to strive for things in life, I will miss some, but I will also get some. It's the getting that keeps me going. The second reason I shared those stories is to inspire you to train yourself to be what I call a "Forward Mover." That means always to move forward. Too many people desire great things but have developed a habit of always not attempting and of staying put where it is safe. By going forward you train your body and mind

If you do the smart things now, you will complete the Ph.D. degree

to always move in the direction that you desire. Doing it my way, you will experience lots of failures in your life; however, you will experience some victories that really matter. **<u>You Need To Develop The Habit Of Moving Forward.</u>** As a kid I used to say take a chance. So take chances in your life, and success will show up all around you.

I hope you were inspired by me sharing my Michael Jackson and Arnold Swarznegger stories. I'm sure as you look back over your younger years (or even now) you can find something about which you were fearless or some great thing that you imagined achieving. Therefore, as doctoral students you must stay hungry. You must propel yourself. Most important, you must never throw in the towel and give up.

Hot Points

Identify important information that you need to refer back to.

_____

_____

_____

_____

_____

_____

_____

_____

If you do the smart things now, you will complete the Ph.D. degree

Chapter 10

Dissertation Tips

"Don't let the fear of the time it will take to accomplish something stand in the way of your doing it. The time will pass anyway; we might just as well put that passing time to the best possible use."
Earl Nightingale

"Keep away from people who try to belittle your ambitions. Small people always do that, but the really great make you feel that you, too, can become great."
Mark Twain

The dissertation is not something that Ph.D. students have to dread if they start off on the right foot. It is something that you should look forward to and really enjoy. Good preparation is the key. Good preparation deals with time and being consistent. Those who fumble the ball here are those who did not use their time wisely.

Because I have my Ph.D., that means I'm "really smart" and can make up words that are not in any dictionary. I coined the term "disserphobia" a few years ago. It refers to one who has an irrational fear of the dissertation and will do anything and everything to stay away from it. To my knowledge, I am the originator of the word and I'm going to propose to Webster's Dictionary that it be added in their next edition. The dissertation

198

should be viewed as something to look forward to. Too many students don't pursue the Ph.D. because of the many ghost stories that they have heard regarding the dissertation; I equate it to the passing of the Bar for law students. Many graduate students have such a fear of the dissertation that they join "groups." These groups are comprised of Ph.D. students who seek help to handle the stress. Although I'm not against one seeking therapeutic help if needed, it is quite interesting to me that these groups are so very necessary for many. I've even discovered therapeutic groups via the Internet for students working on their dissertation. There are self help and therapeutic books written specifically for graduate students experiencing stress while working on their dissertation. That's amazing!!! **You can succeed and complete your dissertation without therapy.**

No one wants to invest time, energy, and money into four to seven years of Ph.D. work and end up not finishing the dissertation or what we affectionately call ABD (All But Dissertation). In short, we can define the dissertation as an investigation into an area put into book form. Simple enough. So, when should you begin working on the dissertation? Well, the average Ph.D. student will complete all of her course work, complete qualifying exams (if required), develop a dissertation proposal (if required) submit it for approval, and then after all that, she will start working on her dissertation. That is not a wise approach to starting the dissertation. This chapter is not a chapter on how to write your full dissertation, but rather some suggested ideas on what you can feasibly do in the first eighteen months of your Ph.D. program. Normally, most of what you do regarding the dissertation will come after completing all your course work and any qualifying exams. However, you can start on the project and get a large chunk done in the first year and a half putting you on track to finish the dissertation and graduate in a reasonable time. Upon entering your Ph.D. program, you need to keep in mind that your end goal is to walk down the path of completing the dissertation and graduating. Am I right?

I want to introduce to you five dissertation tips that will keep you focused and headed in the right direction. Although there is variation in different programs, I believe that these tips are universal and apply to any major or program.

Tip #1   Choosing a Topic

Typically upon entering a doctoral program many students will already have an idea of or may be close to deciding what their interests are for a dissertation topic. If you already know what it is that you want to do, then, discuss your interests with a trusted advisor. However, if you are like me when I entered my program,

If you do the smart things now, you will complete the Ph.D. degree

you have no idea what it is you want to do. If that is the case, then here are some ideas. Review scholarly research journals in your major area. In reviewing journals you will see what others are doing in your area and often times some research being done will spark an interest in you, leading you to discover other related areas that may develop into your dissertation topic.

A second suggestion would be to review completed dissertations in your campus library from your particular area. Again you will see what others have done and through that spark an area of interest within you. Another suggestion would be to review some published work of your professors. This way you get to see what they have done and what their interests are. Also, as you review their work, develop questions and talk with them about their work. Your professors will be pleased that you have taken an interest in their work. Doing this can often lead to a dissertation topic. Additionally, talk to trusted professors about a potential topic. Ask them what may be a good dissertation topic for you. It is important that you begin to seek your area of interests early in the game (inside of your first year) and start developing it. Remember this: Your dissertation topic does not have to be totally original or perfect. The truth is, nothing is really original and perfect. Keep in mind that it's okay to have a dissertation topic early in your program and change it later. Changing dissertation topics is a very common reality. Also, many students think that whatever their dissertation is on will be their life-long research agenda or work. Not so. The truth is that many of today's professors' current work is totally unrelated to their dissertation topic when they were in graduate school. It is good if your dissertation is expanded upon in your future work, but it is not a life or death thing. Get started early so that you can graduate in a reasonable time.

Tip #2   Review Literature

In your first semester and ongoing semesters, read at least six theoretical and ten empirical studies (from scholarly journals) related to #1 above per month. Once you have found what it is that you want to do for a dissertation, you now must read about every related research in that area that you can find. My dissertation was on mentoring, and my advisor once told me that I need to know every thing about mentoring and to read about every mentoring program ever done. I thought that was impossible. It would take me twenty years just to scratch the surface. However, I did spend a huge amount of time reading abstracts (a short summary of a study, usually one to two pages) on every study I could find related to mentoring since that was going to be my dissertation. My advisor also told me that it's never acceptable to complete a dissertation and to go before your committee for your defense, having omitted an important study or finding in that area. So read, read, read, read, and read.

Additionally, you want to organize a system that will make your life easier down the road. Make a filing system and arrange the theoretical and empirical studies in a separate file. As you develop your dissertation and especially your literature review section, you will need to refer to these articles over and over again. Also, set up sub-categories of the articles to specify type of studies. Remember you are doing this now (in your first semester), not down the road.

Tip #3   Review Dissertations

Now, you have your topic (tip #1), and you are reading several theoretical and several empirical studies monthly (tip #2). You are well on your way to knowing a great deal about your area of interest. Tip #3 is fun and quite simple. Begin to review completed dissertations from your university campus library, especially from your particular college and department. Note the following as you review them:

- Sections of the dissertation
- Arrangements of the chapters
- Writing styles

- Number of total pages
- What's included

No one is born knowing how to write a dissertation or the content of a dissertation. Believe it or not, since the beginning of time, every Ph.D. recipient, including your "smartest" professor, has reviewed completed dissertations from the library to learn what it is and what's inside of it. Early as a graduate student, I literally reviewed more than 2000 dissertations in the university libraries and other local universities' libraries. Don't read an entire dissertation, just review and scan them. You want to learn how they are put together. I noticed that most dissertations have five chapters with very similar sections, and chapter arrangements. As I reviewed them, I noticed that some of them were five hundred to twelve hundred pages in length. Pressure, Pressure, and more Pressure. I thought WOW, I can't do this. However, I was relieved that most of them averaged about 120 pages. After reviewing and scanning more than two thousand dissertations, I felt very comfortable in my ability to complete this formidable task.

If you do the smart things now, you will complete the Ph.D. degree

Tip #4   Dissertation Proposal

Now you have your topic (tip #1), you are reviewing six theoretical and ten empirical studies every month (tip #2), and you are reviewing and scanning dissertations (tip #3). You are well on your way. Tip #4 should be done after your first year and the beginning of your second year. Start your second year off by reviewing sample dissertation proposals. A dissertation proposal is a brief summary (five to fifteen pages) of what you plan to do. These may not be readily available, so you will have to inquire about them from your department or ask your advisor how to do one. Typically, it includes a summary of a short literature review, explanations of procedures to carry out, information on subject used if any, type of design, and the type of research methods to be employed. Reviewing these samples from your department will help you in forming your proposal. Getting this done is a major step forward. Too many students wait until they have completed their course work and qualifying exams before starting this. Do this at the start of your second year if there are no departmental rules against it. Next, share your proposal with a trusted advisor in your department. Have your advisor to answer these three key questions.

1. **Is this a feasible (or doable) study?** *You want to know can this be done, and whether it can be done in a reasonable time.*

2. **Is this a study that is likely to be accepted by my not-yet-developed dissertation committee?** *You want to know if a dissertation committee will allow you to do this study.*

3. **What changes, if any, can be made in this proposal to make it an even better study?** *You are solidifying what you are doing.*

After making any revisions to your proposal as suggested by your advisor and getting his or her favorable responses to the revision, make a suggestion to your advisor regarding a second reviewer and have that person to review it as well. After making any and all necessary revisions that are favorable to both, have them to tentatively sign off on it as an acknowledgment of a good prospective for your dissertation. Note, although you may be some time away in actually forming your dissertation committee, it is very important that these two individuals who gave you the approval be strong candidates to be on your dissertation committee, with at least one serving as chair of the committee. Getting early approval of your proposal will eliminate some problems down the road.

Tip #5   Begin Writing _____

Around the eighteenth month of your program, begin writing your literature review. Normally there are five chapters in a dissertation. The literature review (usually chapter 2) is the section that you want to write first. If you have been actively doing tip #2 and #3, this process of writing will be easy and flow smoothly. As you review dissertations from your library, you will observe that this section is typically the longest. It requires many hours of reviewing different types of related literature. However, you are far ahead of most because you started reading the literature early in your program.

Getting started with these tips will put you on the path to completing your dissertation in a reasonable time. So start with tip #1 now.

Hot Points

Identify important information that you need to refer back to.

_____

_____

_____

_____

_____

_____

_____

_____

Chapter 11

Seven Virtues of Successful Graduate Students

"Most of the important things in the world have been
achieved by people who have kept on trying when
there seemed to be no hope at all."
Dale Carnegie

"Nothing great was ever achieved without enthusiasm."
Ralph Waldo Emerson

"Only those who dare to fail greatly can ever achieve greatly."
Robert F. Kennedy

I'm defining a virtue as an inner quality that exists inside some people that gives them the edge in high achievement. Positive thinking is a virtue. You're heard the old saying, "Is the glass half empty or half full?" A progressive and positive thinker would say it's half full. This person has a positive outlook on life. This person strives for excellence and will not accept average in his life. For many years, I made a standard for my life based on a quote I heard from George Burns. He said, "I would rather fail at something I love, than to succeed at something I hate." Most people are succeeding every day at something they hate. They set their alarm clocks to wake them up early in the morning. It goes off. They hit the snooze button for another fifteen minutes of sleep. Then they get up and dress themselves, go to work to a job they hate, get off at 5:00 o'clock. They drive home in bumper to bumper traffic, arrive home around 5:30 p.m. if the traffic was not heavy; eat dinner at 6:30 pm, watch television till bedtime, and get up again the next day and do the same routine. They look forward to Fridays (affectionately called TGIF or Thank God It's Friday), weekends, and their once-a-year vacations.

To be a winner in life you have to live by George Burn's statement. Your poor background, lack of money, or lack of experience shouldn't be allowed to be a factor if you plan to win in life. I came from a background that exemplifies poverty and lack; no one could have predicted that I would have achieved academically or in providing quality self-help materials on a national level. In life, I'm winning because I've learned some virtues that were not inherited nor in my genes.

The seven virtues that one needs to be successful in a Ph.D. program are discipline, focus, patience, motivation, mental ability, networking ability, and positive thinking. I will explain each virtue in detail. Your task is to evaluate yourself to determine if you have them all. If you don't possess them, you can develop them through the tips that I will offer.

Discipline

To be disciplined is to be in control. Your behaviors and mind set must be geared towards completing your program. You have to have a "stick-to-it" mind set. That means delaying some things while you work on the important things. During the 6 ½ years of working on my doctorate, watching television was rare. I mentioned television specifically because it is the number one destroyer of getting important things done. I was determined to succeed. Discipline includes following instructions, staying focused, and most important it means NOT GIVING UP no matter what! Evaluate yourself; are you a person of disciplined behaviors? These behaviors are something that you can learn and improve upon.

Focus

For more than twenty years I have studied the lives of successful people. Those who have excelled as business owners, corporate executives, athletes, and great academicians all posses the ability to stay focused. John Maxwell said that "focused thinking harnesses energy toward a desired goal." A person who isn't focused is like a ship without a rudder; the rudder is the apparatus that controls the direction of the ship. The ship will go in any direction the wind blows without a proper working rudder. Unfocused people are like that ship; they move on a whim and are easily distracted, especially when they experience set backs.

If you do the smart things now, you will complete the Ph.D. degree

Several years ago while working on my master's degree, I was working two jobs and was involved with lots of extra curricular and social activities. One of the jobs was a night job working from midnight to 8:00 am. Because of these work hours and all of the other activities that I was involved in, I got off focus. My grades went south, and I was placed on academic probation with one semester to bring the grades up, or else. Getting off focus is easy to do when you are in graduate school. So at the start of the next semester, I made some major adjustments in my life; that is, I eliminated some things to get back on track. It's important that as a Ph.D. student you keep your eyes on the goal; having your attention and time on too many other things will distract you and knock you off course. When I think of being distracted, I think of a lion trainer in the cage with a lion at the circus. In the cage you will observe the trainer of average size and weight with a whip and a small foot stool with a lion weighing about ten times the weight of the trainer. The trainer uses the whip to make the lion move and the stool to make the lion back away. That always amazed me. How can something as simple as a small stool make the massive man-eating lion back away? Certainly the lion could easily overtake the trainer with the whip and stool and devour him for lunch. Here's what I've noticed about the small stool. Usually it has three or four short legs on it. The trainer points it in the direction of the lion, and the lion backs away. The legs on the stool are distractions for the lion. The animal will take his eyes and attention away from the target (the man) and begin to focus on the legs of the stool, and as the trainer moves the stool in a circular motion, it confuses the animal even more. The same is true in life. When we have so many things going on or if we allow all of life's problems to get in the way (such as financial difficulties, family problems, jobs, poor relationships, etc.), these things become like the stool in the lion's cage defocusing us from the goal on which we should be focusing on. As a Ph.D. student, it's important that you stay focused. Don't allow a poor grade on a paper to distract you; don't allow a bad relationship with a professor to distract you; don't allow life challenges to distract you, but keep your eyes and attention on the goal of earning your doctorate degree.

When I was admitted into my Ph.D. program, I did something to help me stay focused. Some may say, "Well, that is a silly thing to do," but I just didn't care. Here's what I did. In 1996, I started my Ph.D. program. Immediately, I got on the computer and I made myself a Ph.D. diploma and posted a date on it to be achieved in four years, dated in the future for August 2000. I bought a cheap frame from the local Wal-Mart, hung it up on the wall in my home above the desk where I was going to do my studying. Therefore, I couldn't help but notice it everyday. See the following copy:

The University of Alabama

Has conferred upon

Samuel Earl Jones

The degree of

Doctor of Philosophy

In

PSYCHOLOGY

Goal Completion Date: _____ August 2000 _____

_____ August 1996 _____

Samuel E. Jones   Today's Date

My signature on this document represents a commitment to finish and graduate

Making yourself a diploma now, putting it in a nice frame and placing it in a location that you view daily may appear silly, but it can help you to stay focused and motivated by seeing it everyday. Paul J. Meyer said that "what ever you vividly imagine, ardently desire, sincerely believe, and enthusiastically act upon, will come to pass." Vividly looking at the diploma on the wall daily will strengthen the desire within you and drive you towards completion. If you can't see it, then you can't have it. You need to see the finished product in your hands now. Students around the country who have attended my workshops are advised to make the diploma NOW and hang it on the wall. By the way, this writing down your goal can apply to anything you want to achieve.

Patience

Patience is a virtue that brings about understanding and wisdom. It is the ability to wait and not be overly anxious. It helps you to think things out before acting too hastily, making costly mistakes. An impatient person will make mistakes before a patient person. For example, in the second year of my doctoral studies I exhibited impatience in an important area that cost me some relationships. I developed a topic and a plan on what I was going to do for my dissertation. My mind was made up; I was happy, excited, thrilled, enthusiastic, inspired, and I felt like I could leap over tall buildings. Through my excitement and zeal, I went about sharing too much information with too many of the wrong people.

Because I moved too fast without thinking, I ended up hurt and hurting other people. I learned patience from that negative experience. Wisdom in that situation would have been to wait, ask questions, get information, and only talk to the key players.

Motivation

Please allow me to bring out the psychology in me for a moment. Motivation refers to the physiological and psychological factors that cause us to act in a specific way at a particular time. If you are a motivated person, you will show these three characteristics: you are energized to do something, you direct your energies toward a specific goal, and you have intense feelings about reaching that goal. Let's break down the three:

Energized to do something

To be energized means to do it when you don't feel like doing it. Do it even when you don't want to do it. You just do it because it's important. Remember the bunny from the battery commercial; it just keeps going, and going, and going. To be successful in graduate school and in life, "YOU Incorporated" have to keep going and going and going. Even when times look dark and gloomy, you don't allow what's going on to stop you. One way that I keep myself motivated is being accountable to at least four close and trusted friends. I share my goals with them and ask them to check on me periodically (every month) on where I am in reaching the goal. By doing this I stay motivated to get things

If you do the smart things now, you will complete the Ph.D. degree

done. I never wanted these four individuals to call me for a goal status and I be caught off guard by getting nothing done.

Think hard for a moment and identify four significant, intimate, and trusted individuals (i.e., spouse, friend, relative, classmates) and list their names below. Ask these individuals to commit to contacting you periodically to check on your progress.

Four People

Name _____

Name _____

Name _____

Name _____

Directed energies toward a specific goal
Motivated people are goal-oriented. They live life on purpose. To live life on purpose means that every thing you do, you do it with an intended outcome. Motivated people set goals all of the time. Directing energies toward a specific goal occurs when one is physically and psychologically driven towards something that will literally consume the body and mind until that goal is materialized.

If you do the smart things now, you will complete the Ph.D. degree

Three things have helped me to stay directed towards my goal. Do these three things, and you will see a difference as you work towards your doctorate:

#1

First, I determine from inside of me what I'm excited about and what I really want. It must be something that is extremely meaningful, worthwhile, and unless I pursue it, I will not be happy. I call this **Intrinsic Desire**.

#2

Second, I visualize myself with this item, position, etc. in hand. Then I get a picture of it. For the purpose of this book, I made a diploma of the aforementioned Ph.D. and hung it on the wall so that I could see the product daily. This works for anything; for your dream home or dream car. Get a picture of it and place it somewhere and view it daily. It works for relationships. Write out on a piece of paper what qualities you want to possess and view them every day.

#3

Plan of Action. Having a desire for something, visualizing it, and looking at a picture of it is useless unless you have a plan to get or have it. I'm not the smartest person in the world, and I don't like trying to come up with a successful plan if there is a model of success already available. Why try to reinvent the wheel if the current wheel is working fine? Develop a plan of action by looking at or getting information on what has worked in the past. I'm a believer in having models and mentors available to help me. I'm never afraid to ask for help or directions from anyone who has already achieved what I want. Go to people, get information and find what works and develop your specific plan of action around that information. But wait!!!!.....you may say. I don't know anyone who has achieved in an area that I want to achieve in, so what do I do? I'm glad you asked. I had a desire to get completely out of debt. However, I didn't know anyone personally who had achieved that status and was living an abundant life. I know lots of people who are living abundantly with material things, but they go into deep debt in order to live with abundance. I began to search for an answer, and through networking and talking to others I came across this book titled The Total Money Makeover written by nationally syndicated radio personality and financial advisor Dave Ramsey. Although I don't know this man personally, he still is a model and mentor for me. After reading his book a few years ago, I took the very practical information and developed a Plan of Action to meet the goal. So, everything you need to know is out there; you just have to go get it.

Intense Feelings About Reaching the Goal

This is the last area of the necessary characteristics in a motivated person. Intense feelings are synonymous with passion. I looked up the word passion in the dictionary and it used words like "strong feelings," "outburst of emotions," and "lust" to define passion. Those are all good definitions. However , since I am a doctor and I have a Ph.D., I am going to make up my own definition for the word. You too can do this when you graduate with your Ph.D.

My definition of passion is:

when external situations or circumstances trigger the hypothalamus part of your brain, it causes your body to experience strong love or hate towards the situations or circumstances that drives you to get something in your life or get something out of your life.

WOW, what a powerful definition of passion. To be motivated and to win in life, you need to feel that way about reaching your goals. Ethical people who have intense feelings or are passionate about something are willing to do whatever it takes that's morally right to achieve the goal. If you come from a background similar to my own, then you don't have an option; YOU MUST BE PASSIONATE ABOUT EARNING YOUR PH.D. Otherwise, you are just spinning your wheels and wasting your time. You might as well go back to doing what you've been doing. A movie produced by Mel Gibson a few years ago, titled The Passion of the Christ showed what a man would go through who has deep passion about someone or something. Strong hate was the intense feeling that drove me to complete graduate school. I hated my present job, I hated my current status in life, and I couldn't live happily unless I changed it. There is no special formula or assignment that I can give you that will help you to develop this. The truth is, we all have passion about something or someone. You have to find it.

If you take on these three behavior characteristics—1) being energized to do something, 2) directing energies toward a goal and 3) developing a plan of action toward directing your energies toward a specific goal, you will achieve it.

Mental Ability

Your mental health/strength will be challenged as you work towards completing your Ph.D. degree. Mental ability is having the skills to handle stress, problems, setbacks, and unexpected challenges. I have observed Ph.D. students who had challenges to occur during their matriculation and literally became sick. They were overwhelmed with their personal problems and the challenges of doing their school work to the point in which it became overbearing. Doctoral students must learn to handle anything that life throws at them during their matriculation. If you can't handle life challenges, you will eventually give up and not reach your goal. You can train your mind and body to be strong. Let's take a simple mental ability test. Answer the questions below:

If you do the smart things now, you will complete the Ph.D. degree

222

Question	Yes	No
1. Do you frequently feel like you can't cope with everything you have to do?		
2. Do you frequently feel like your life is rush, rush, and more rush?		
3. Do you normally get angry when you are kept waiting?		
4. Are you described by others as one who blows up easily?		
5. Do you frequently feel like there is only one way to do something?		
6. Are you easily irritated?		
7. Do you frequently complain about things that have happened in the past?		
8. Do you tend to make a big deal out of small things?		
9. When stuck in traffic, do you get angry?		
10. Do you often feel like if you want something done right, you might as well do it yourself?		

If you answered three or more of the questions with a "yes," then you may be a person who allows life's obstacles to get in the way. You need to work on strengthening your mental abilities. Three things have worked for me; they are as follows:

1) Viewing obstacles and problems as small stuff and choosing not to let them bother me.

2) Reading and listening to inspirational material.

If you do the smart things now, you will complete the Ph.D. degree

3) Exercising and eating good nutritional meals.

The interesting thing about problems or setbacks is that you have to choose to allow those things to mess with your mind. I believe that when we focus on and constantly think about past situations, this thinking builds on that, and gets in the way of our success. You have to accept the truth, and the truth is your past mistakes, failures, people who have hurt you, and current obstacles are just "small stuff," and you will keep going with a positive attitude no matter what.

Network

To network is to go about meeting people and locating information that helps you along the way. As a Ph.D. student you need to extend yourself. Let's face it. This is a new venture for you, and there is much to know. If you are quiet, introverted and a loner, you may miss out on opportunities, or you may not succeed in graduate school. You need to interact and seek assistance from other people. This virtue will help you to gain resources, and gain people to be on your side, as well as gaining information, positions, and monies. You should never stop networking. Continue to network after you graduate. But as a new graduate student, there are at least four primary areas for you to begin networking in now. These four areas are 1) get to know key people (i.e., professors, administrators, staff personnel) and their functions or roles, 2) campus and off campus organizations that are relevant to your specific area, 3) resources, and 4) information about teaching and research assistantships. It's important that you be a person who goes about looking for information and talking to people.

Positive Thinker

I saved the best for last. Without a doubt, the most important virtue that you need is to be a positive thinker. A short definition of a positive thinker is one who *always looks for the best*. Another meaning would describe a positive thinker as *one who lives a lifestyle of always attending to the positive, and when faced with negatives is one who always looks at the potential possibilities that others can not see.* Take the positive thinker test to see where you are.

Positive Thinker Test

1. When I fail at something, I tend to look for the next opportunity.
2. I think this positive thinking stuff is valuable and worthwhile.
3. When I fail at something, I will usually keep at it until I succeed.
4. I have recovered from the last major setback in my life.
5. Those closest to me would describe me as a positive thinker.

6. Usually, I stick with a goal even if I'm not seeing results.

7. I have great expectations for my future.

8. On a "happiness" scale of 1 to 10 with 10 being the highest, I am between 9 and 10.

9. I get excited about difficult tasks and challenges.

10. I view myself as a winner.

11. Others often come to me for advice.

12. My confidence in my abilities is high.

A positive thinking person would have answered the questions above with a "yes." If you answered "no" to any of the items, then you need to go back and change your thinking in that area by replacing it with a positive even if you don't feel it.

Positive thinking needs to be a way of life. Most of us who have been there will agree that a Ph.D. program is not a Ph.D. program unless it includes some things that are bad and some things or situations that will set you back. We would also agree that the dissertation writing is not a dissertation writing unless you experience some "bads" and some "negatives." So you need to expect this. John Maxwell said that "the difference between unsuccessful people and successful people is how they view failure." To be successful it is essential that you not view failure as negative, but rather focus on the potentials within it.

In my developing years, and I must say that my developing years are a continuing process for me, in the early 90's I went to Los Angeles to hear Les Brown speak. I was extremely impressed by how he spoke about his many failed marriages. I have seen divorce and bad relationships destroy people and graduate students alike. At that meeting and recently divorced again, Les Brown said that "I'm going to get married again and I'm going to keep doing it until I get it right." I was inspired by his tenacity and positive views on marriage. Unfortunately, too many people think negatively about marriage after going through a bitter divorce. Bitter, divorced women say things like "I'll never trust another man again; all of them are no good." Bitter, divorced men say things like "all women are after one thing," or "they can't be trusted."

I wasn't always a positive thinker. I had to learn to develop my mind to think that way. I thought I had it all together until a few years ago when I learned that I'm vulnerable to allow bad situations to override my positive thinking. Here's a situation that occurred a few years ago which took some extra time for me to overcome. I had a friend named Darryl with whom I would have trusted my life to be in his hands. This person to me was more than a brother. Our friendship extended over twenty years. I contacted Darryl at his Florida residence to get his opinion on something that he specialized in— real estate investment properties. A few days later, Darryl phoned me and offered to sell me a duplex property, one of many that he owned located in Florida. The appraisal that he had showed a value of $110,000. He explained to me that the property was in very good condition with many improvements and located in a nice area. He said that both units had good-paying tenants; that he would assist me with identifying and locating a management firm to handle running it, and agreed to assist me with everything I needed. He convinced me that it would be a good monthly income and a good investment for future resale.

Without checking everything out and without going to Florida to view the property for myself, I put my complete trust in him and his word, bought the property for $100,000, believing that I had some $10,000 equity and two good paying tenants. Upon taking ownership, and to my shock and amazement, I learned that my good friend had lied and deceived me. The appraised value of $110,000 was a fraud. I contacted several different agents in the Florida area and learned that the true value of the property was around $45,000 to $50,000. Through telephone contact with several real estate agents and property management companies who visited the property on my behalf, I learned that the condition of the property was bad and needing many repairs. Also, I learned that the community was a very bad community infested with gangs, drugs, and a recent killing next to the property had just taken place prior to my buying it. Additionally, only one unit had a tenant in it and the other was vacant and vandalized. The one tenant was a bad tenant who refused to pay his rent. I was completely stunned and absolutely speechless as I began to take in all of this. It really, really hurt to be taken advantage of by someone that I considered to be my best friend. Needless to say, I lost a great deal of money in repairs, struggled paying the mortgage, and the property went into collections. To compound the problem, during that time I was writing my dissertation, my wife and I were expecting our second child in a few days. I was under lots of pressure to meet our financial needs, under pressure to complete my dissertation, and trying to maintain my sanity during the coming days of having our baby.

I just couldn't stop there with my friend. I needed to know more about this person whom I trusted all those years. Through further investigation, I contacted those who had done business with him and learned much more about him and his way of doing business. Some of those who were working with him described him as a "slick talker" and said that he was up to taking advantage of people through buying very bad properties, inflating the values and selling them. I began to do a wide investigation of the property that I bought which included contacting the individual whom Darryl bought the property from. The man was shocked when he learned that I paid $100,000 for a piece of junk. In his own words, he said, "How could that #@$%**%*(#@ (words I can't repeat) sell you that dump for that amount of money? HE USED YOU for his own gain!!" The man also told me that he bought the property from the city, paying only $10,000 for it. After making some minor improvements, it was worth about $38,000, and he sold it to Darryl for about $40,000. I've never met this man, but through the tone and volume of his voice, I could tell he was more upset than I was. He was down right angry that I was taken advantage of. I also learned from him and other documents that Darryl did not own the property for the length of time that he told me. Actually, he sold it to me days after acquiring it himself.

After learning this information, I contacted my friend by telephone and shared with him my disgust at what he had done and how he had lied to me. As I expected, he denied having knowledge of just about everything that I shared with him. It was apparent that I was not going to get anywhere in trying to talk with him, so I decided to take my loss and deal with it. I could clearly see the evidence of the other individuals whom I communicated with in Florida who described him as "up to no good" and a "slick talker."

My thoughts on this situation and the person whom I trusted for many years went to the bottom of the pit. For several weeks, I experienced hurt and anger like I've never experienced before in my life. I wanted to give up completing my dissertation and go do something else. However, I knew giving up would be a bad decision, and I realized that it was my own fault for not visiting the property and for not checking everything out before buying it. The lesson I learned was that that was just too much trust to place in an individual. After the monies lost and after the law suit and foreclosure, I eventually pulled myself together. How did I pull myself together? Well, I began to look for positives that I could find in that situation, and here's what I found. These may not appear to be positives, but, anytime you learn and grow from an experience, it's positive.

#1 I learned the importance of how to be involved in business transactions.

#2 I learned that an abundance of money received by a person can bring out the true character of that person. *Note: money doesn't change people; it brings out and magnifies what's already in the person.*

#3 I learned to take responsibility for my inaction in the decision that I made.

Upon looking at that situation positively, I was able to move on and complete my dissertation and enjoy the arrival of our baby.

As you go about graduate school, it's important that you not allow negative situations, events, and circumstances to side track your progress. No matter how bad, LOOK FOR THE GOOD IN EVERY SITUATION. A positive attitude with a desire to succeed in spite of challenges must be a part of "you" for the next several years. Challenges will come your way. You will want to stop or give up. You will want to call it quits. So it's crucial that you stay focused and keep the goal in your mind. Make a commitment to yourself and to a close love one that you will go all the way and complete your Ph.D. degree. When times are tough, go back and view information that you learned from this chapter. Remember, you have come this far; keep moving forward and the reward will come.

I congratulate you on coming this far. So continue to propel yourself, and you will reach and obtain all of your goals. You have my best wishes.

If you do the smart things now, you will complete the Ph.D. degree

Hot Points

Identify important information that you need to refer back to.

_____

_____

_____

_____

_____

_____

_____

_____

_____

If you do the smart things now, you will complete the Ph.D. degree

If you do the smart things now, you will complete the Ph.D. degree

Chapter 12

Life for you is just beginning

"No one is here by accident. You are not a mistake, a
miscalculation or a product of chance. Everyone who
has been born has a purpose, and that includes you. You
may have to discover what that purpose is, but it's in you."
Sharon Williams

There is an old saying that goes like this;

*One day a farmer's donkey fell down into a well. The
animal cried piteously for hours as the farmer tried to figure out
what to do. Finally, he decided the animal was old, and the well
needed to be covered up anyway; it just wasn't worth it to retrieve
the donkey. He invited all his neighbors to come over and help
him. They all grabbed a shovel and began to shovel dirt into the
well. At first, the donkey realized what was happening and cried
horribly. Then, to everyone's amazement he quieted down. A few
shovel loads later, the farmer looked down the well. He was
astonished at what he saw. With each shovel of dirt that hit his
back, the donkey was doing something amazing. He would shake it
off and take a step up. As the farmer's neighbors continued to
shovel dirt on top of the animal, he would shake it off and take a*

step up. Pretty soon, everyone was amazed as the donkey stepped up over the edge of the well and happily trotted off! The moral of the story is that life is going to shovel dirt on you, all kinds of dirt. The trick to getting out of the well is to shake it off and take a step up. Each of our troubles is a stepping stone. We can get out of the deepest wells just by not stopping, never giving up!! Shake it off and take a step up.

During this journey of working towards your Ph.D. or any goal you want to accomplish, you are going to have some dirt shoveled on you. Obstacles are going to come, challenges will present themselves, people won't support you, and bad things will happen. You have to remember five simple rules:

1. Free your heart from what you have done to hurt others or what others have done to you – Forgive.
2. Free your mind from worries - Most never happen.
3. No matter what hand you were dealt in life, live to do your best and appreciate what you have.
4. Give more than you expect in return.
5. Expect less from people but more from yourself.

Thinking about my own journey, I have had difficult challenges to come my way, some were even self-imposed through my own stupidity. We all make bad decisions, do stupid things, and fall into traps. Some people stay in traps or wells and never get out or recover. It's important that you have an attitude and mindset that keeps you going. My favorite quote is by George Burns, who said, "I would rather fail at something that I love, than to succeed at what I hate." Most people are succeeding at doing something that they hate. It's really not success or succeeding, it is that they have adapted to being content through habit or inertia (nothing changing unless some velocity or force occurs). Burns' words have directed my life.

The Bible teaches us that "Faith is confidence in what we hope for and assurance about what we do not see (NIV; Hebrews 11:1)." To me, this faith and confidence mean to act like you belong, act like you have "it" already, act like you are in charge of your destiny, and always move through life with boldness and assurance of success. You cannot allow things, people, or events to stop you from pursuing your goals; too much is at stake. Sometimes you may have to go at it alone without any support.

I have developed an attitude over the years of going for my dreams in life; not just earning the highest degree offered at universities, but striving to make a difference beyond academic achievement. Sometimes, individuals examine their life and believe that the bad events that have occurred or are occurring will determine their future. You are the one who makes the choice on this matter. Currently, I have a private practice in the mental health field. Here are the top ten challenges that people are experiencing everywhere:

> Death of a love one
>
> Major disease or illnesses (mental and physical)
>
> Divorce or failed relationships
>
> Financial disaster (job lost, bankruptcy)
>
> Major family conflict
>
> Served time in prison
>
> Drug addiction
>
> Physical, emotional or sexual abuse
>
> Loss of self esteem

All of those can inflict major changes in anyone's life. But it doesn't have to stop you. Disagree with me if you choose, but I believe that the "loss of self-esteem" is the biggest loss on the list. Self-esteem is how you feel about yourself and the value you place upon yourself, which determines how you respond to challenges in life and how well you recover and move forward. My own view of life and living is related to my death. What am I talking about with this life related to death? Well, as a Christian, I believe that when I die, I will see God and spend eternity in a place called Heaven. The child in me tends to think that when I die and go to Heaven that God will reveal to me all the things I could have done, and the differences I could have made while living on Earth. I dread the thought of not doing everything that He has put before me or the things He would have wanted me to do especially as it relates to making a difference in the lives of people.

Years ago, sometime in the late 1980's, I lost my job, was making poor grades in college, was not able to keep my apartment and was having the most challenging time. During that time, I attended an event to hear a well- known speaker in Los Angeles. I remember the speaker making these comments. "Life is God's gift to you and what you do with your life is your gift to God." He also said, "When I die, I want to be used up, and don't want to take anything with me to his grave." Upon hearing that speech, my life changed. I started attending workshops on growth, self-esteem, and development; learning from some of the top professionals in the country. I listened to tapes, attended workshops, and read everything I could find to develop myself. After learning growth principles, I began to practice those principles in the real world; engaging in challenges that made no sense for one to engage in who has a background such as mine.

I started reading my Bible daily. My life verse in the Bible was Romans 12:12; which says, "be joyful in hope, patient in affliction, and faithful in prayer." The words hope, patient, and faithful are critical to your success. Hope is the feeling that what is wanted can be had or that events will turn out for the best. Patient is bearing pains or trials calmly or without complaint while in a difficult situation. To be faithful is to be steady in allegiance, strict or thorough in the performance of duty. That speaker in Los

Angeles gave me hope, taught me patience, and to be faithful, because it's now important to me to use the gift(s) that God gave me. I don't want to go to heaven and be shown the difference that I could have made while living on Earth. This needs to be your attitude and way of thinking. You must strive for excellence.

Too often we read something inspiring or attend an inspiring seminar or workshop and don't put the information learned into action. As you have noted, throughout this book, I attempted to have you to interact with the material in a practical manner leading to action and success. Now, I want to give you some _Life Changing Principles_ (LCP) that will have an impact on you and the lives of others you touch. If you commit and do the ten life changing principles listed below things will began to happen in your life that you never expected:

LCP #1 - Meet and make two new acquaintances per month for six months = 12 people.

WHY LCP#1- We limit ourselves by staying in our comfort zone. Reaching out and meeting others in your locality is dynamic in the sense that you never know what others can bring into your life or how you can help them. Personally, I have gained much by approaching people whom I don't know and showing an interest in what they are doing.

LCP #2 - Go back to anyone and all whom have offended you and to those whom you have offended and ask for forgiveness.

WHY LCP #2 – Whether you are the victim or the offender it is critical to your success that matters be cleared up. When you are holding on to "un-forgiveness issues" a debt is left unpaid and it affects you whether knowingly or unknowingly in your thinking and in your heart and soul. Your success in life is connected to freed-up thoughts, heart, and soul. Not to mention your integrity.

LCP #3 - Give away two gifts per month to someone unrelated to you.

WHY LCP #3 – Giving is the hallmark to making a difference in the lives of others as well as yourself. The concept of giving and receiving actually works. There are many in religious settings and other settings who teach that if you give them or their organization some money, then you will get some money back (sowing and reaping). Personally I disagree with that form of manipulation and trickery. My concept of giving (sowing) and receiving (reaping) is different. This life changing principle is not about your getting some money back because you gave some money. But rather, when you give, you are making a difference in the lives of someone and you are receiving the benefit of knowing that you are making a difference in the lives of people. In other words, your benefits in giving are (a) helping others, (b) increasing your self-esteem, (c) feeling good about yourself, and (d) life satisfaction.

If you do the smart things now, you will complete the Ph.D. degree

242

Whether you give money or other gifts, don't enter a habit of giving with expectations of getting money or material gifts back. More than ten years ago, my wife, kids and I were having dinner at one of our favorite seafood restaurants in an expensive area of town. We noticed near our table were acquaintance of ours. Having a meal at that particular restaurant for us was an infrequent experience because we couldn't really afford it. After the meal and waiting for the waiter to bring the expense report, she approached us and shared that someone paid for our meal. To this very day, I am grateful to the person who paid for our meal, and I will never forget that act of kindness. I do suggest you give money or gift cards because people's needs tend to be in those areas. It can be $10 cash or even a $10 gas gift card. The receiver of your gift will always be appreciative and will never forget you. If money is an issue in giving, then you can give your time, goods or services, your expertise in some area, or just some random acts of kindness. This life changing principle will have an effect on your life.

LCP #4 - Apply for six scholarships that you think that you do not qualify for or four jobs that you think you do not meet the qualifications for.

WHY LCP #4 – You may ask, why should I apply for something that I know I don't meet the qualifications for, or that I know that I won't get? My answer to those questions is another question.

If you do the smart things now, you will complete the Ph.D. degree

How do you KNOW that you won't get it? And, what is the worst thing that could happen if you sought something and didn't get it? I have learned the importance of raising the attention of others who don't expect their attention to be raised. In the 1970's there was movie that aired starring Burt Reynolds (known as the Bandit) in "Smokey and the Bandit." There was a classic line that the Bandit spoke to his co-host in trying to convince him to drive his 18-wheeler across state line to deliver hundreds of cases of beer (which was against the law). The co-host said, "we can't do that, it's against the law and it has never been done." Reynolds responded and said, "that's because you and I have never done it before." Then Reynolds gave that classic line and said **"we never not yet done it have we."** That may be bad English, but the thought behind that line is powerful. He was communicating that they haven't done it, which means that they haven't failed at it. You get it? If you don't try, you don't fail; allow yourself to fail. There are some hard and difficult things in life that you have never done, but those same hard and difficult things have "never not yet been done by you." So go for it. Applying for things you don't qualify for (scholarships, jobs, and positions) brings about so much development. It doesn't matter whether or not you get it, but what does matter is how it helps your development and how it creates a mind set to go for things in life. This LCP changes your attitude and aptitude on what you believe is possible. The year before I started my Ph.D. program, I collected over 300 businesses, institutions, and organizations' addresses. Then, I sent all of them, all 300 plus of them a letter requesting funding for my education. You never know what you can achieve in life unless you "GO FOR IT."

LCP #5 - Search the Internet and locate "movers and shakers." CEO's in the business world, successful authors, academic leaders, entrepreneurs, professional speakers, media personalities, then get their mailing addresses and send them the following letter:

Hello Mr./Ms. Whoever,

My name is Jane Doe and I reside in Anywhere, State. I'm writing you because I have learned about the work that you have done and the ongoing contributions that you are making. Although we have never met, for years, I have admired your work. It has impacted my life so much. For example (give an example). I am very interested and passionate about what you are doing. Chances are I will never meet you. But I wanted to express how excited I am with what I have learned from you. Currently, I am (add whatever you are doing that's related to this person). We may never meet, but you are an inspiration to me.

Thank you,
Your signature

Include your contact information in the letter!

WHY LCP #5 – Haven't you admired someone because of their work? Of course you have. It may be a famous author, cooperate

If you do the smart things now, you will complete the Ph.D. degree

executive, business owner, U.S. President, academic leader, famous athlete, popular television chef, or radio or television personality. Many of us have been impacted in some way by a well-known personality or famous person. The purpose of reaching out again is that you never know what opportunities may come your way through this small effort of sending letters to someone admiring their work. I am speaking from experience. I have written the owner of the Los Angeles Lakers, Oprah Winfrey, politicians, Dave Ramsey, and a host of others. In the movie "Shawshank Redemption," a prisoner wrote hundreds of letters to the state governor all were ignored for years, but he continued to write and later received what he was asking for. You have nothing to lose by using the sample letter above and sending it to people who are movers and shakers in the world; but everything to gain.

LCP #6 - Take a different driving route to home, school, work, or wherever you go than you would normally take.

WHY LCP #6 – This is a simple life changing principle to complete. But it is important. I have so much experience with this principle through driving alone and sometimes with my family. There are times in which I have my wife and kids in the car and instead of taking the shortest and quickest route to our home, I'll take a detour traveling the longest route to home just to explore my surroundings and to introduce myself to an area that I haven't seen before. Through my wife surprise, she would say "why are you going this way, it will take longer to get home." Although I understand her frustration, my goal is to see a new place - consisting of possible new business or residential development, and just maybe, coming across an opportunity that can lead to something that I would not have seen had I not taken that route.

LCP #7- Make your-self available to someone and mentor him/her (this could be a young person, undergraduate student, colleague, a couple with problems, or almost anyone)

WHY LCP #7 – This LCP should be obvious and easy to see. Every reader of this book has some talents and gifts. Too often, people think that they have nothing to give to others in the area of mentoring and grooming someone's development. Remember the Bible story (Matthew 25:15) in which there were three servants; one was given five talents, another two talents, and another one talent. The two who had the most talents invested them and increased their investments by 100%. You may believe that you don't have five talents or ten talents, but you have something. My belief is this, if you have air to breath and blood flowing through your veins, then you can help someone through mentoring. You do have some knowledge even if it's life experience. You can motivate someone. Examine your pass failures and mistakes to help someone to not make the same mistakes. There is a benefit that you receive from mentoring someone. That benefit is life satisfaction in impacting your legacy through someone, not to mention increased self-esteem.

LCP #8 - Ask someone who is smarter than you to mentor you. **WHY LCP #8 -** This is also obvious as far as an important life changing principle. No matter how old you are today, on the day that you were born you needed to be mentored or cared for. That doesn't stop just because you are an adult. You should have a mind-set of always wanting to learn from others who are smarter than you or has some specific knowledge in an area that you lack. This person can move you along your path in life. Additionally, I believe that we all need someone to be accountable to. This accountability that you give to this person or mentor gives him or her permission to inquire about your doings and your not doings. In other words, you need someone to keep you on target in all areas of your life including your academics, your career moves, your relationships, your finances, and so much more. I heard someone recently give a talk on how dangerous it is for you to only know what you are going through, we all need someone to talk to, to help or guide us. This mentor you select should be someone who is mature and cares about you.

LCP #9 - Read any three of the underlined books this year on personal development; <u>Unlimited Power</u>, and/or <u>Awaken the</u>

Giant Within both by Anthony Robins, Thinking for a Change by John Maxwell, The Art of Closing the Sale and/or Maximum Achievement both by Brian Tracy, Live Your Dreams by Les Brown, The Psychology of Winning by Denis Waitley, The Total Money Makeover by Dave Ramsey, The Power of Positive Thinking by Norman Vincent Peal, and Epistles by Paul (Bible).

WHY LCP #9 – I have read all of the books listed above. Reading and practicing the principles you learn will make a difference in your life. Not to sound vain, but I can honestly say that I am a product of the good that I have learned from Anthony Robins, John Maxwell, Brian Tracy, Les Brown, Denis Waitley, Dave Ramsey, Norman Vincent Peal, and Paul's Epistles. My self-esteem, my pursuit of excellence, my personal beliefs, my passions to help others, my spiritual growth, my beliefs about money and giving, and my belief in my ability to impact the world are all related to information I have learned from these authors. Some experts suggest that one should read a book a month (12 books in a year). Well, that sounds admirable, but the truth is, reading that much may have a negative effect. The goal would become accumulating having read lots of books, and not learning and developing. Don't try to increase your number of books read for the sake of reading. Let's be real, it takes time to soak information in and utilize it. A comfortable amount is three books in 12 months. Then as you read, start practicing the principles you learn from the readings. If you keep with this LCP, you will see a tremendous difference in your self-esteem, confidence, and willingness to try big things in life.

LCP #10 - At least five days per week, wake up in the morning and do some self-talk or positive affirmations. Below is an example of my personal self-talk—words of affirmation that I speak out verbally while looking in the mirror, driving my car, and often silently while I'm alone or during my down time.

"I am Samuel Jones, I am a great person, I'm good looking, I'm smart, I'm a winner. I have lots of gifts and talents to share with others. I have a great mind and a giving heart. I learn from others who are smarter than me. I do not accept defeat, I am a winner, I am a mover and I continue to move forward. I always give a 100% of myself, nothing can stop me, today I am going to make a difference."

Use my "words of affirmation" or develop your own. Then speak it to yourself on a daily basis. It will have an impact on your attitude, your beliefs, and your actions.

WHY LCP #10 - Believe it or not, you are speaking negative or positive affirmations every day. Most of the time, you are speaking to yourself unconsciously or silently. For example, negative silent speech may include saying things like:

> I can't do that
>
> It won't work for me
>
> I shouldn't approach that person
>
> I never will be able to (fill in the blank)
>
> I will always be in this position

When we communicate that way to ourselves it affects everything about us. Refuse to talk or think negative about yourself, but rather talk to yourself this way:

> I can
>
> It will work for me
>
> I should approach that person today
>
> I will be able to (fill in the blank)
>
> I will be in a position to succeed

Ongoing internal self-talk is critical to how you feel, think, believe, and act. Why not start speaking positive affirmations? Try it for six months. You will begin to see a difference along the way like you have never seen before.

Each of the life changing principles above is intended to create personal development within you and others around you.

If you do the smart things now, you will complete the Ph.D. degree

They will create open doors of opportunities that will come your way. Trust me!! Your life will never be the same. It is so important that you not miss out on this opportunity. Do the ten principles now and you will see things taking place in your life that you never dreamed of! Trust me!!

Make the quote below your life statement and live that way.

"I would rather fail at something that I love, than to succeed at what I hate." George Burns

Hot Points

Identify important information that you need to refer back to.

_____

_____

_____

_____

_____

_____

_____

If you do the smart things now, you will complete the Ph.D. degree

About the Author

Dr. Samuel Jones is a marital therapist, motivational speaker, and workshop presenter. Dr. Jones has been in the helping profession for more than 20 years. He has worked in radio and television. Dr. Jones and his wife live near Birmingham, Alabama with their four children. As an author and speaker he uses his gifts to assist and give guidance to children and adults in areas of their lives related to education, family relations, career, and reaching personal goals. He is a sought after speaker and is requested around the country to share his experience and knowledge with others. Dr. Jones believes that no matter what hand one has been dealt in life that every person has the potential to achieve beyond their expectations.